C000181052

# SUPERSTITIONS
## Folk Magic in Hull's Fishing Community

by
### ALEC GILL

HUTTON PRESS
1993

Published by the Hutton Press Ltd.
130 Canada Drive, Cherry Burton, Beverley,
North Humberside HU17 7SB

Copyright © 1993

No part of this book may be reproduced, stored in a retrieval system or
transmitted in any form, or by any means electronic, mechanical,
photocopying, recording or otherwise without the prior permission of
the Publisher and the Copyright holders.

Printed and bound by

Clifford Ward & Co. (Bridlington) Ltd.
55 West Street, Bridlington, East Yorkshire,
YO15 3DZ

ISBN 1 872167 56 X

# CONTENTS

## PART FOUR — OBJECTS

## PART FIVE — 'FEAR OF THE GODS'

## DEDICATION

*Dedicated, once again, to
Audrey Dunne.*

*Coming from East Hull,
you don't believe
in any superstitions.*

*That's fine –
but 'Thanks' for
believing in me.*

# ACKNOWLEDGEMENTS

Mildred Abbott, Rennie Acum, Peter Adamson, Joyce Allan, Jim Anderson, Brenda Andrews, Paul Armstrong, Frances Ashfield, Jack Athelton, Charles Ayre, Gordon Baker, Eileen Barker. Evelyn Bateman, Ron Bateman, Arthur Beal, Geoff Bell, Mike Bell, Gary Bennett, Len Berner, Ernie & Lillian Bilocca, Brenda Black, George Bleasby, Pam Blowman, Alan Bower, Ellen Brocklebanks, Gillian Brown, Ron Buckley, Dave Bucknall, Margaret Burwell, John Calvin, Ethel Cardwell, Len Carr, Tom Carroll, Edith, Brian & Margaret Casey, Arthur & Marian Chambers, Diane Chapman, Elsie & Jeff Chappell, Edna Clarke, Derek Coates, Carol Coiffait, Hilda Collins, Sylvia Cook, Joe Cooper, Leslie Copeman, Arthur Cowan, Andrina Cowie, Arthur Credland, John Crimlis, Freya Cross, Jill Crowther, Sheila Dagett, Deborah Dalton, Mike Dash, Ron Davig, Pat Davy, Betty Dawson, Alan & Sylvia Day, Joe de Gournai, Mary Denness, George Dickinson, Dorothy Dobson, Sara Donaldson, Maggie Doyle, Liz Drewery, Dennis Duerden, Annie & John Duffin, John Dunn, Audrey Dunne, Geoff & Ivy Edwards, Rob & Pat Ellis, Leonard Enevoldson, Irene Everitt, Stan Fairbrass, Freda Fee, Elsie Fisher, Olive Fisher, Phil Fisher, Doreen & George Fleet, George & Maureen Flitton, Adam Fowler, Andrew Foxon, Flora Franks, Jim Fuller, Stan & Evelyn Futty, Bernard Gerrard, Maria Gerrard, Norma & Clarrie Glenton, Ann Glentworth, Violet Goodrick, Audrey Grady, Jean Gray, Kathleen Gray, Sarah Gray, Tricia & Eva Gray, Florence Greenfield, Jonathan Grobler, Sally Haden, Ron Haines, Harold Hall, Terry Hannis, Lynn & Victor Harbord Snr. & Jnr., Chris Hardy, Sue Harmer, Les Harrington, Hella Harris, Annie & John Harrison, Brian Hawkins, Richard Hayton, Hilary Henrickson, Grace & Robert Hilton, Paul Hilton, Ted Hodgson, Edna & Bill Holcroft, Les Hollome, Frances Hook, Ray Hotham, Edna & Fred Houghton, Sue, Edith & Sid Hunt, Alf Ireland, Dick Jackson, Jack Johnson, Jean Johnson, Raymond & Linda Johnson, Ron & Pauline Johnson, Audrey & Ron Jones, Cordelia Jones, Eric Kendall, Chris Ketchell, Ken Knox, Terry Layden, Edna Leake, Jean Leathley, Bill Lewis, Martin Liddle, Betty Lloyd, Jill Long, Mary Longden, Alf Louth, Clara & Tom Magee, Marjorie Major, Florence Marshall, Kevin Marshall, Cora Mason, Kenneth McAll, Brian & Shirley McCoy, Liz McClory, Gordon Meredith, Gladys Minter, Audrey Moore, Herbert Mortimer, Debbie Moss, Bonita Musgreaves, Mavis Newman, Ted Newman, Carole Newton, Peter Nicholson, Charlie O'Neill, Bill O'Pray, Jean Owst, Doris Palmer, George & Dorothy Palmer, Tom Parkinson, Jenny & John Pattison, Nan Pattison, Louis Pearlman, Vernon Phillips, Lily Plant, Leslie, Lillian & David Powell, Guy Putnam, Wendy Quinney, Marjorie Ragglett, Robert Ramsbottom, Val Rendall, Vera Riches, Richard Rilatt, Ted & Laura Rilatt, George Ritchie, Joe Robinson, Bob Rowntree, Ron Sayers, Mike Scrimshaw, Dorothy Sharples, Dora Sherman, Brian Sitch, Edith & Neil Smith, Lucy Smith, Susan Smith, Carrie Smithson, Mary & Harry Spaven, Audrey Spencer, Madge Stark, Beryl Stephenson, David, Stephen & Christina Stipetic, Alf Stockdale, Bill Storr,

Thomson Stott, Ernie Suddaby, Margaret & Brian Tate, Dick Taylor, Jim & Lorraine Taylor, Madge Taylor, Pauline Taylor, Richard & Barbara Taylor, Christine & Peter Thackray, Terry Thresh, Lily Thurston, Marion Toffolo, Dora Tulip, Vera Turnbull, Alf Turner, Terry Uden, Wilf Vines, William Ward, Eric Wedge, Mavis & Roy Wegg, Maise Weightman, Jean Welbourne, George & Evelyn Wells, Valerie & George West, Olive Westcott, Christine & John Wheeler, Samantha White, Paul Whiting, Clarrie Wilcockson, Geoff & Graham Wilkinson, Dave & Shirley Williams, Evelyn Williams, Jim Williams, Maureen, Eileen & Shaun Williams, Joyce Williamson, Francis Wilson, Jean Wilson, Lily Wilson, Robert Wise, Robert Wisepart, Helen Wootten, Eileen Wright, Ursula Wright.

## ABBREVIATIONS

| A. | — | Aberdeen registered trawler |
|---|---|---|
| AD | — | Anno Domini (In the year of our Lord — After Christ) |
| BC | — | Before (the birth of) Christ |
| c. | — | circa. / around that time |
| Ch. | — | Chapter (referring reader to another part of the book) |
| GY. | — | Grimsby registered trawler |
| H. | — | Hull registered trawler |
| HDM | — | *Hull Daily Mail* |
| H.M.T. | — | His Majesty's Trawler |
| Ibid. | — | as previous quotation |
| LO. | — | London registered trawler |
| p. | — | page number |
| pp. | — | part pages |
| Rev. | — | Reverend |
| RNMDSF | — | Royal National Mission to Deep Sea Fishermen |
| s.s. | — | Steam ship |
| Supt. | — | Superintendent of the RNMDSF |
| WWI | — | World War One |
| WWII | — | World War Two |

## SYSTEM OF DATES

| Text | = | 26 January 1955 |
|---|---|---|
| Newspapers | = | 26 Jan. 55 |
| Others | = | Jan. 1955 |
| Interviews | = | 11/92 |

# INTRODUCTION

SAYING: *Of all seafarers there are none more
superstitious than fishermen.*

This book grew out of curiosity. Historically, fishermen and religion go together. The disciples of Christ were 'fishers of men'. Continental fishermen request a Catholic priest to bless their boat. Scottish fishermen were not keen to work on Sundays. And the Yorkshire fishermen of Filey were strong Methodists noted for their singing. I was, therefore, keen to establish the beliefs of Hull trawlermen and their families.

From Day One of interviewing Hessle Roaders I asked about their religious beliefs. I naïvely assumed it would be easy to find if they were church- or chapel-goers; and how involved they were with Hull's Fishermen's Bethel or the Royal National Mission to Deep Sea Fishermen. But, to my surprise, I kept getting nothing tangible back. Apart, that is, from the fact that the local Sunday Schools were jam-packed. Adult attendance, however, revealed a different picture.

The Hessle Road traders and middle-class professionals, in the past, preferred the Anglican churches. Generally, the railway families flocked to the numerous chapels, especially during the early days of Primitive Methodism (pre-WWI). The non-denominational Bethel (and more recently the Mission) was in close contact with the fishing families. The minister had the unenviable task of 'breaking the news' to a fisherman's wife that her man was lost at sea — and he later held a special Memorial Service for the crew.

But that seemed the limit of contact between the places of worship and the fishing families. Except, that is, for the three major 'rites of passage': birth, marriage and death. This is not to say that the people did not believe in God — but that their spiritual needs were met in other ways. I gradually began to realise that the people did not conform to my pre-set expectations — they were not regular worshippers — so I dropped this line of research! Being a local historian, it is one thing to describe factual events (lost Hull trawlers), but completely different to get into the realm of beliefs.

What the Hessle Roaders did tell me about, however, was their susperstitions. Initially, I did the predictable thing and took little notice — not uttering taboo words seemed strange, and their old-time practices seemed a dying legacy which was out-of-place in the modern world. But taboo tales kept being repeated, new ones came my way, and variations of old ones caught my imagination. It slowly dawned that the Hessle Roaders' 'spiritual vacuum' was, and still is to some extent, satisfied by ancient folk beliefs.

Then, suddenly, I began to write them down. I had to. Taboos were the pivotal point of some trawling yarns. Curiosity turned to fascination. Fascination became a passion. When I mentioned to group speaker-finders of a new topic to my list of talks — *SUPERSTITIONS: Silly or Serious?* — they

*Cordelia Jones (née Brown) is a gold-mine of Hessle Road folklore and she usually has a nice tale related to each belief. As a young girl she was brought up mainly by her grandmother Sarah Taylor at No.76 Manchester Street. Cordelia was born in 1912 and grew up during the dark days of the First World War. She soon learned that "Everything was good luck or bad luck" – especially when lightning flashed over the city (Ch. 21). This is Cordelia in November 1935 playing her accordion.*
Courtesy Marion Toffolo.

eagerly booked it. The first guinea-pig group being the NALGO Retired Members' Section at the Hull Guildhall (Jul. 1990). The join-in talk really took off and testified to a wide interest in this irrational subject. The floodgates then opened with one story triggering off various other anecdotes from the audience. My strict criterion for whether or not I wrote them down was if they had a strong trawling link. Obviously, during my talks, people mentioned superstitions from rural areas, cargo ships, East Hull, and elsewhere —but these were not recorded. My source material for this book comes from Hessle Roaders and their relatives. It is worth stressing that the book is not about general maritime taboos. Whenever a related example comes from, say, Brixham, Scotland or Brittany, this is clearly stated in the text. But what must be said, is that although the superstitions spring solely from Hull, they nevertheless tap a source of belief which is universal (and, perhaps, eternal).

Over two hundred and fifty people contributed to this work (see Acknowledgements). But two in particular provided a wide range of examples. Cordelia Jones has a fountain of stories. She was raised by her Grandmother Sarah Taylor to whom "everything was good luck or bad luck". And Mary Spaven is the only Hessle Roader I know who has written down various superstitions. I first came across her 32-item list at the Hull Heritage Centre in 1984. The organisers, however, did not know the compiler. An accidental meeting with Mary's daughter — Val Rendall, one of my psychology students —put us in touch. Mary collected her material from the Alexandra pub on Hessle Road, and her own story is in 'Born with a Caul' (Ch. 2).

Each interview led to others. There was no shortage of people to contact and, unfortunately, I never got around to see everyone. My notes grew and grew. From being a passive paddler on the shore of spiritual beliefs, I began to swim in a sea of superstition. I soon realised that these deep waters had strong undercurrents and an occasional shark. Turbulence came from many quarters — warning me not to get out of my depth.

*Many people deny being superstitious. Little research has been done to find what
percentage perform the ancient rituals. Gustav Jahoda (1969), however, cited an experiment
in the USA which showed that 72 percent of pedestrians stepped out onto a busy road
rather than walk underneath a ladder. There was no painter working up the ladder
and its feet rested in the kerb.
For 15 minutes observers recorded 51 people approach. A total of 37 chose
to expose themselves to the dangerous traffic, while only 14 walked underneath (p.26).
This chap on Hessle Road also superstitiously, and awkwardly,
avoids the feared ladder.*
Copyright Alec Gill.

Common sense classes superstition as stupid. Science has no time for
irrationality. But what it fails to notice is that no matter how often it is shot
dead by logic, superstition has a habit of being born again. The Church is both
antagonistic and ambivalent. Theologically, it is bound to clash with any act of
faith which fails to comply with its own. One believer's religion is another's
superstition — and vice versa. Yet there are some within the Church who have
tried, over the centuries, to account for the taboos as if they had originated
from Scripture. Their half-hearted attempts were always doomed to fail. In the
process, however, they added confusion to the conflict.

Even academia gives a mixed message. According to one respected authority
on superstition and fishing, there were no such beliefs in 20th century Hull.

Peter Anson (1965), in his book *Fisher Folk Lore*, wrote about the time when North Sea trawlers changed over to steam-power after 1880, and how Hull and Grimsby crewmen acquired "comfortable homes". He then deducted that "old customs, taboos and superstitions were forgotten, or deliberately ignored, if they were remembered, for they belonged to a way of life that it was better to forget" (p.39). False views like this go some way to explain why this topic is rarely researched. Other academic sources, however, are more encouraging. Jahoda (1969), in his book *The Psychology of Superstition*. pointed out that surveys of the general population fail to measure people's true feelings about superstition. And that future research needs to focus upon jobs "involving risk, uncertainty or fear... As far as I know there are no systematic studies of the differential incidence of superstition for people in different occupations" (p.128). Although Jahoda did not inspire the present work, hopefully, its findings will make a small contribution to his appeal.

Sociologically, Hessle Road is an ideal culture within which to study any beliefs. A few of the remarkable features about Hull's fishing families are that they were primarily working class, academic achievement had limited social status, it was a close-knit community, there was a high-risk of unemployment due to social and health factors (accidents at sea), they had a precarious livelihood, a man sometimes 'landed in debt' to the trawler owners, the men were away from home for long spells with only short stays ashore, deep-sea trawling was classed as 'an extreme occupation', there was a high death rate (for every coal-mining fatality, there were over four fishermen killed — Holland-Martin, 1969, pp.134-35), the shadow of death loomed over the community, a wife never knew when she might become a widow, and there was a strong matriarchy to support a woman in distress. There were other special features of this unique breed, but these will unfold as we delve into the mystical side of their lives. A back-drop to this dynamic culture is that Hull was 'the greatest deep-sea trawling port in the world'. The purpose of this book is not to pass judgement on whether superstitions are right or wrong. They exist and influence people's attitudes and behaviour. They are a fascinating social and psychological phenomena.

The lack of serious research into folk superstition also reflects a social-class bias toward working people. This conclusion is not new. In 1725 the Italian philosopher Vico was disturbed by "the negative view always taken by the upper classes" toward folklore traditions and that "uniform ideas originating among entire peoples unknown to each other must have a common ground of truth" (Birlea, 1987, p.363).

Set against this background of conflict and confusion from academia, clergy and the powers-that-be, is the vast quantity and quality of material gathered from the fishing families themselves. As my oldest interviewee, Ursula Wright (102), said about superstitions, "there are thousands of 'em". I needed to strike a balance between the family anecdotes and the research literature. Few Hessle Roaders knew where the taboos originated. Clarrie Wilcockson expressed the popular view that "everybody in the fishing fraternity is superstitious — don't do this, don't say so-and-so — it's just *tradition*". In order to find the source of these *traditions* I was forced to turn to various dictionaries, pre-historical texts,

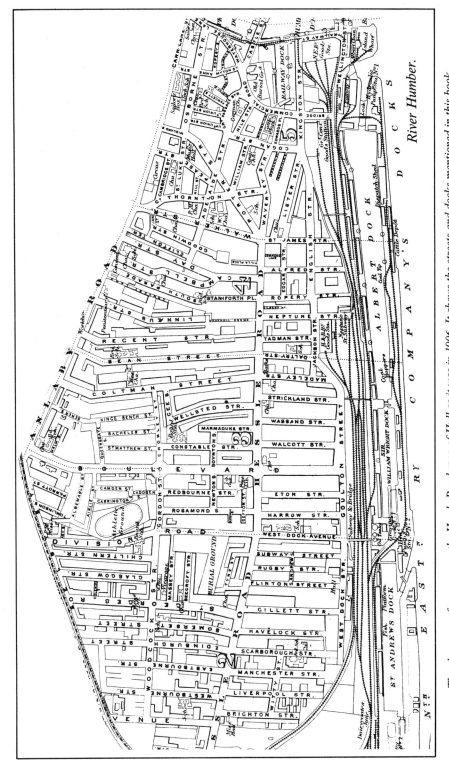

*The above map focuses upon the Hessle Road area of Hull as it was in 1906. It shows the streets and docks mentioned in this book.*
*Courtesy G. W. Bacon.*

Greek myths, biblical sources, theories of magic, occult material, witchcraft, anthropology, psychology, and different encyclopedias. The *New Encyclopædia Britannica* (1979 — Vol. 9, pp.684) showed the breadth of superstitious belief throughout the world. A brief extract follows [with Hessle Road examples added in square brackets]: Many beliefs are universal [evil eye] and timeless [lucky charms] others are found in certain countries [black cat] or communities [Hessle Road], some are peculiar to specific social or vocational groups [Arctic trawling] and people develop their own personal superstitions [a skipper's lucky cap].

Indeed, radio operator Ron Haines said, "I've sailed with thousands of trawlermen and most have some pet superstition". Patterns of belief varied from family to family. Each household had certain taboos while being ignorant of others. Some people, of course, had no time for superstition. It seems that superstitions are things people do rather than something they talk about — a sub-cultural practice. In many respects, the taboos were so taken-for-granted that some Hessle Roaders did not realise that they were superstitious. Mary Spaven's comment was, "I did not think I was superstitious until I moved over to East Hull". Taboos swim below the surface. Personally, I do not consider myself as a superstitious person. I do not carry a lucky charm or throw salt over my shoulder, and I walk under ladders (sometimes). But I do like to say 'White Rabbits' on the first of each month, enjoy breaking a wishbone, seem forever to be 'touching wood', and am pleased if someone wishes me 'Good Luck' —therefore, I do superstitious rituals without feeling myself to be a superstitious person.

The diversity of anecdotal material and academic research needed to be structured into book form. I had a rough idea what to do, but was delighted to find a precedent in the work of Wundt (1921). In his book *Elements of Folk Psychology*, he focused upon three broad categories: Folk, Animal, and Object. With a little bit of juggling around I was able to slot each belief into one of these groupings. Initially, I thought that the three classes would in turn divide into two sub-sections with stories from Ashore and Afloat. This worked well for the Folk part with women in the community and men at sea — so much so that these became Parts One and Two respectively. But this neat split broke down when it came to the Animal and Object taboos (Parts Three and Four). Anecdotes about birds, for example, flutter between land and sea — likewise with food and colour magic. So at the end of the day, the superstitions are presented in four main parts: Folk (Ashore), Folk (Afloat), Animals, and Objects — a more detailed outline is listed on the Contents page.

Part Five, the final one, is special. But it may well be 'putting the cart before the horse'. I am going against my university training which adamantly stated that 'Defining the Subject' must be outlined first. Five is the 'Why' part of the book — the theory bit. The first four parts address practical issues like *what* the superstitions are, *when* they happen, *who* they affect, *how* they unfold, *which* animals and objects are magical, and from *where* the beliefs arise. By presenting material in this order, I hope to expose non-Hull readers to these colourful beliefs without an explanation of 'why'. For this is how the Hessle Roaders themselves encountered the rituals.

Part Five is, for me, the most exciting. It attempts to stand back and look at why primitive thinking is still strong in the age of science. In summary, 'Fear of the Gods' provides definitions of key terms such as 'folk magic'. Other chapters look at Psychology, Hunt Magic, Luck, and Occult aspects. The next three chapters unearth the historical roots with an examination of the Pagans, Women, and Fatalism — before the book ends with a Concluding section. Overall, the work divides into thirty-five Chapters, plus sub-sections where necessary.

There are less illustrations in this book than in any of my previous four publications. One reason being that it is difficult to photograph superstitions in action — but hopefully, the range of material conveys a feel for the Hessle Roader's unique way of life. The major reason for less pictures is to allow more space for words — there is so much to say on this intriguing topic.

The following complete quotation, from a short *Hull Daily Mail* article highlights a sailing-day dilemma for one Hull trawlerman:

### Failed to Sail: Had Superstition

"Because he had a superstitious feeling something was going to happen at home, George Edward Morgan (31) fisherman of Worcester Terrace, Gillett Street failed to sail after signing on the *Kingston Galena* [H.217].

For wilful disobedience to a lawful command he was fined £1 and cost in Hull today.

Mr. T. H. Jackson prosecuting said that Morgan had been up for a similar offence in 1939"

(HDM 15 Jan.49).

# PART ONE
## FOLK (ASHORE):
## Women in Community

### Chapter 1
### SAILING DAY

HESSLE ROAD SAYING:
*Never wash on sailing day,*
*Or you'll wash your man away.*

Sailing-day was a whirl-pool of superstition. Fishing families drifted along on a torrent of do's and don'ts. Taboos affected both men and women — and provide an invaluable insight into their relationship. Five strict sailing-day superstitions were:

* A woman must *not* wash clothes the day her man sails; otherwise "He'll be washed overboard".

* *Never* wave a trawlerman off or a 'wave' will sweep him off the deck.

* He must *never* look back or return home once outside the house.

* *No one* said 'Good-bye' — it is too final and he may never be seen again.

* Women were strictly *taboo* on the fish dock at high tide when trawlers were due to set sail for the Arctic waters.

Sailing-day superstitions are saturated with magical ritual (Ch.27). Women ashore and men afloat unwittingly performed a 'rite of passage' as a crewman set off to sea. Older women instructed younger ones, "Never *wash* the day he sails. You'll *wash* him away!".

The naïve logic which underlies this non-washing ritual is based on the belief that our dirty clothes possess our spiritual essence (Radford, 1974, p.351). And if this spirit is washed out at the critical time of embarking upon a perilous Arctic trip, then that person is washed out of the family too. At the more sinister level, the very act of pushing a man's garment under water is similar to plunging him under water too. In other words, it mimics the action of drowning him. To avoid this accidental imitation, therefore, the trawlerman's clothes (and all the family's washing) were not done at that sensitive time.

It is when these old sailing-day taboos are broken that interesting tales emerge. On a lighter and sceptical note, a woman told me at a talk that she really did not like her husband — "we were always at each other's throat". So she deliberately washed his clothes every time he set sail — hoping he would be washed out of her life. Asked if he was ever washed overboard, she begrudgingly said, to the amusement of the audience, "No! It didn't work — unfortunately".

Not waving a trawlerman off follows a similar imitative principle. But Jill Long impulsively did this when her (first) husband Tony Harrison set off on 16 November 1966 for a pre-Christmas trip aboard the freezer trawler *St. Finbarr* (H.308). Jill recalls how, "It was in the early hours of the morning and, I don't know why but, I pulled back the curtains and waved him good-bye. Tony saw me, looked back, and waved too". Jill was born into a fishing family and

*Three of the Hull trawlermen lost during the Christmas blaze aboard **St. Finbarr** (H.308) are shown here having a farewell drink, just before their fatal trip, at the Maybury Pub (Maybury Road). Tony Harrison (left) is with two mates David Young and Kenny Pullen (far right), along with their girl-friends (Nov. 1966). Jill Harrison is in the centre of the group.*

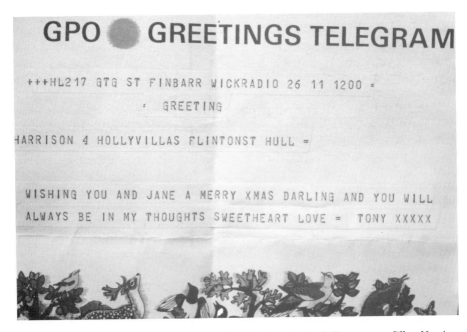

## GPO ● GREETINGS TELEGRAM

```
+++HL217 GTG ST FINBARR WICKRADIO 26 11 1200 =
              GREETING

HARRISON 4 HOLLYVILLAS FLINTONST HULL =


WISHING YOU AND JANE A MERRY XMAS DARLING AND YOU WILL
ALWAYS BE IN MY THOUGHTS SWEETHEART LOVE = TONY XXXXX
```

*Below is the final Christmas telegram (via Wick Radio, Scotland) Tony sent to Jill at No. 4 Holly Villas, Flinton Street – not far from the fish docks.*
Courtesy Jill Long.

followed all the superstitious routines, especially on sailing day. It was, therefore, unusual for her to wave her husband off. But, she had the urge and just did it. That was the last time she ever saw him.

The superstitious signs had already been bad for that trip even before Tony left his Flinton Street terrace home. Three times the owners (Hamlings) sent a telegram to cancel the voyage: "Don't sail on a.m. tide — Report for new orders". Fellow crewman Brian Williams took this triple delay as an ill-omen and refused to sail on the *Finbarr* — Brian was lucky that time (but Fate had other plans for him — Ch.16).

The 1139-ton freezer was barely two-years old and this was only her fourteenth trip. The Atlantic fishing off Labrador (Canada) took longer than planned and the 25-man crew were disappointed to learn that they would not be home for Christmas as expected. Tony sent a seasonal telegram to Jill and their ten-month old baby Jane. Jill replied with a coded message. Tony understood that if ever his wife signed her name 'JILLIAN', it meant she was pregnant.

The weather was so bad on Christmas Eve that Skipper Thomas Sawyer ceased fishing and allowed his crew time off to relax and enjoy themselves. Around 7.30 a.m. on Christmas Day fire broke out in the crew's accommodation deck (presumably from an electrical fault). Fierce flames spread at an alarming rate. There was "a sudden expansion of hot air from the accommodation below [which] blew out the doors and shattered the windows of the wheelhouse" (Board of Trade Inquiry, Sep. 1967, No.S478, p.2). The May Day call was answered straight away by the *Orsino* (H.410). Thirteen men were rescued, but sparehand Tony Harrison (20) was amongst the twelve burnt to death (and was to go down with the ship two days later while being towed toward Canada by the *Orsino*).

Jill had decided, with Tony away at sea, to spend Christmas with her parents. She remembers Christmas Day very well because of its ominous links with fire — and commented that "everything happens in threes". Her parents have an open coal-fire and the chimney caught alight that morning. It was not a serious blaze and dad soon got it under control. Later that day, as mam cooked the Christmas Dinner she burnt her arm. News about the third fire-related incident was to come when the Mission Men finally traced Jill at her parents' house.

It was Boxing Day morning when they called to break the news. Jill, was in the middle of bathing her little girl at the time "when I got the knock at the door, I just knew something was wrong". She recalls, "there is nothing anyone can do, it's a way of life when you are married to a fisherman". Jill was the youngest *Finbarr* widow. Seven months later, when her second daughter was born, she named her 'Toni'.

Once a crewman set foot outside the house, it was very unlucky to call out after him. If he 'looked back' that placed him in mortal danger at sea. The never-look-back taboo is universal. The story of Lot's wife in the Bible is well known. Against dire warnings, she glanced back at the damned city of Sodom and was instantly turned to a pillar of salt (Genesis 19:26; Luke 17:32). If a deckhand forgot, say, a comb his wife sent a child or neighbour's lad running after him with it. The youngster knew that the crewman must not break his journey. The object was thrust into the man's hand — a bit like in a relay race — as he strode toward the fish dock — and not a word was spoken.

A similar silent sailing-day departure has been observed not only in European cultures such as Scotland, Sweden, and Brittany; but also as far away as New Guinea (Anson, 1932, p.60). The general rule is that no one, especially a woman, should speak to a departing fisherman. Otherwise, if the taboo is broken he will not set sail for a whole day.

Hull wives spoke, but were firmly forbidden on the fish dock to see the men off. Edie Casey sums up this wide-spread Hull taboo by saying, "They loved you to see 'em in, but you never went to see 'em off — that's one thing you must never do!".

Only men were allowed to see the crew off from the quayside. Provided, that is, they *never* uttered the word 'Good-bye'. Acceptable terms were 'So long, Stan!', 'Cherrio', or 'Good-day' — but never the final-sounding 'Good-bye'. Nor did the men shake hands as a farewell gesture. A similar belief was to *never* watch a person disappear out of sight.

Like all superstitions, the one which prevented women going down to the dock has been broken. The following woeful tale centres around the war-time loss of the Hull trawler *Commander Horton* (H.233). One of two new crewmen on board was Ted Randall. He was a factory worker, but decided in April 1941 to try his hand at trawling. His wife was unaware of the sea-going taboos. She

*This picture shows that not all fishing families bothered with the sailing-day taboos. A strict rule was that a female was not allowed on St. Andrew's Dock to see a trawlerman go away to the fishing grounds. Yet here is Elaine Ireland (c.1965) who saw a relative off aboard the* **Cape Tarifa** *(H.584) – seen in the distance steaming down the Humber.*
Courtesy Alf Ireland.

naturally decided to see him off at the lockhead, especially with this being his first trip. Chatting later to her St. Andrew's Street neighbour, Edna Leake, Mrs. Randall commented that "The *Commander Horton* is an old-looking rust tub". Edna's startled response was, "You never went on dock to see 'im off, did you? You're not supposed to do that!". Upon seeing a look of deep anxiety sweep over the poor woman's face, Edna toned down her comments and dismissed them as 'old wives' tales.

But when the 1914-built *Commander Horton* failed to return after the usual three-week fishing trip, the wives began to get worried. The fourth week dragged into the fifth, and by the sixth the women expected a visit from the minister of the Fishermen's Bethel — to 'break the news'. When Pastor Tom Chappell arrived on Edna's doorstep she immediately thought, "This is it". In her widowed years since the *Horton* was mined in the Atlantic off Iceland, Edna finds it difficult to dismiss the superstitious link between a woman going down to see a trawler off and the loss of her beloved Mack.

If ever a woman saw her husband off at the lockpit, the rest of the crew "gave him Hell". It is difficult to know why there was such a taboo against females going down to the quayside. Poet Audrey Dunne, after a dream about women seeing men off at the lockhead, came to the realisation that, "If all the women — with all their adult awareness that the men might not come back, their sadness at parting, their fears, and remembrance of past griefs — went to see the men off, it would be too much for the couple to bear. This wave of emotion would be so strong as to affect the men themselves. The women remind them of love, tenderness, family ties, and sorrow — things they must not dwell upon as they prepare themselves for the harsh, brutal and dangerous conditions of the Arctic waters. There must be no looking back or they might, like Lot's wife, turn into a pillar of salt and be unable to move. Salt dissolves in water" (2/91).

The crew's morale would suffer and the authority of the skipper and trawler owners would be undermined. Added to this, the women themselves might begin to raise too many questions about trawler safety (as did Mrs. Randall about the 28-year old *Commander Horton* — and, in 1968, Lil Bilocca and the Trawlermen's Wives did after Hull's triple trawler tragedy).

There are various stories of drunken trawlerlads who smuggled prostitutes on board trawlers about to leave the dock (one may have been the *Daystar* H.542 around 1960). Sometimes the women were put ashore at Spurn Point via the pilot boat. Sceptics claim that keeping the wives away from the dock was more to conceal the men's infidelity and prevent gossip within the community than it was to do with superstition.

For the wife left alone at home, the superstitious rituals did not end with the departure of their husband. One skipper's wife (in North Ferriby) never moved a single item of his clothing for 24 hours. His suit and things stayed where he discarded them. Otherwise, she felt she was "shooing him out of the house". This sounds like an extension of the 'not washing' (them away) rule. One mother never emptied her son's tab-ends from the ash-trays for three weeks —until he was safely home. Edie Casey told of a pet superstition peculiar to her family. In the 1930s, her father Frank Beckitt was bosun on the trawlers. Whenever he set off to sea, his wife never cleared the ashes from the coal fire at their Wassand Street terrace home. She also never put his suit away nor emptied his ash-tray until the next day. She did this for years, despite jibes from her children.

When a woman was alone in the house, some were unsure "what to do for best" and others "just mooned about". One remedy was to put on a coat and look around the shops on Hessle Road. Or visit mother or a sister for a chat —until the empty feeling disappeared. A Hessle Road woman described her husband's three-week absence like this: "For the first week I missed him. During the second I got into a routine without him. And for the last week I looked forward to him coming home". But whenever he was home any longer than a couple of days, questions were asked like, "When are you off to sea again?".

Another story demonstrates how the ancient sailing-day taboo survives in modern times. Since the decline of Hull's deep-sea fishing industry, many younger trawlermen have found work abroad. One such seafaring job is aboard the oil-rig stand-by ships in the Persian Gulf. The wife of one man told how she "is not bothered when he flies from London Airport to Bahrain. But when I know he is about to set sail, I never wash any clothes... I can't explain, but I never wash the day he sets sail". This suggests that it is not the leaving of home or the journey that motivates the superstition, but a specific fear which relates in some mysterious way to the sea.

There were four sons in the Fulstow family who all went trawling. Mother Beattie had her own special farewell wish as they left their Tadman Street home. If ever she missed them, she got very upset. She worried that something might happen because she had not wished them: "Fair Winds and Safe Returns".

## Chapter 2

## BORN WITH A CAUL

PROVERB: *Better to be born lucky than rich.* (Russian)

The extreme demands of Hull's fishing industry meant that the trawlermen were rarely ashore when their wives gave birth. The average pre-WWII time between trips was a mere thirty-six hours (three tides). The critical life-or-death period of bringing a child into the world obviously attracted many superstitions — before, during, and after 'the happy event'.

It was unlucky to have a pram delivered to the house before the baby itself was safely delivered — that tempted Fate too much. It was lucky for a child to be born at high-tide; but an ill-omen if delivered during the ebb tide. The moon controls the tides and, in folklore, she is referred to as The Great Midwife. Statistics confirm that "the maximum number of births occur just after full moon and the minimum at the new moon" (Walker, 1977, p.24). The average gestation being 'ten lunar months' as opposed to the nine calendar months.

The strongest and strangest of all child-birth omens centres around the caul — "more precious than gold". When it was known that the midwife or doctor was at the point of delivery, neighbours gathered outside the terrace house. They had lots of burning questions: Are mother and child alright? Is it a boy or a girl? Does the child have a caul? If so, is it for sale? Other mystical names for this thin foetal membrane, which occasionally clings to an infant's head, are veil, mask, or silly-how — meaning blessed or holy hood. The belief is that a child born with a veil will never be shipwrecked or drowned.

On 9 June 1965 Mavis Wegg (née Embley) gave birth to Leslie Anthony at Hull's Hedon Road Maternity Hospital. There was quite a commotion because he had a full veil over his head. The Staff Nurse held the treasured caul in her hand and said, "The doctor will like this veil. He's heard about them, but never actually seen one". Exhausted Mavis was suddenly fearful that she might lose the cherished object. She managed to utter the few words, "My husband's a fisherman". That was enough. The theatre staff instantly knew its other significance. The caul was saved for Mavis. Husband Roy, spare-hand aboard the *Bayella* (H.72), was ashore, and he experienced Mavis' labour pains too. Although he was disturbed to see his suffering in these terms, a nurse told him the pains would stop when the baby was born — and they did. Mavis felt "it was an honour to have a child with a veil". When Roy returned to sea and news spread about the caul, he was offered £50 by one man and £100 by another. All offers were flatly refused, of course. Leslie's treasured veil remains one of the most precious possessions of the Wegg family to this day.

There is another Hessle Road caul story from forty years earlier. May Spaven (née Harper) was born in May 1925 at No.9 Myrtle Avenue, off Wellsted Street — her maternal grandmother Fanny Robinson's house Great

21

*This lucky caul belongs to Leslie Wegg – born 9 June 1965. In ancient times folk believed that whoever possessed a caul would not drown. When Leslie's father Roy returned to sea after the delivery, he refused an offer of £100 for it. David Copperfield was not so fortunate in Charles Dickens' book: "I was born with a caul which was advertised for sale at the low price of fifteen guineas. Whether sea-going people were short of money... or short of faith... I don't know" – no one bought it (p.15).*
Courtesy Mavis Wegg.

joy erupted when it was realised that Mary's head was covered with a caul. It was valued over the years. Their good neighbour was a trawlerman named Mr. Bryant. Whenever he returned from the fishing grounds he always sent his wife Annie around with a 'fry of fish' for the Robinson family. These parcels were a regular treat. Then one day in 1930 news came through that his trawler was wrecked at Iceland [this may have been either the *Eske* (H.859) on 1st April or *Lord Fisher* (H.264) on 24th December]. Fortunately, the crew had a lucky escape and returned safely to Hull. When Mr. Bryant arrived home, Mary's mother Olive was so excited to see him alive that she gave him the precious caul for future protection at sea. He was reluctant to take it as a present and offered Olive some of the big (old-fashioned) £5 notes. But she was, by nature, very strong-willed and firmly refused to take a penny. He eventually accepted the caul as a kind gift.

When Grandma Robinson heard that the caul had left her family she was furious. Fanny had a dominant personality and the two women were at logger-heads over Mary's caul. Fanny argued the traditional view that "Anyone born with a caul will never drown as long as it is *kept* in their

22

*Olive Harper (above ) with her three-month old daughter in 1925. When Mary was born with a caul over her head, Grandma Fanny Robinson (right) was highly delighted. She believed in its protective magic. It was carefully wrapped in tissue paper and kept safe in a bedroom drawer. Five years later, Olive gave the caul away to a shipwrecked trawlerman. This caused a big row with her mother. One of Fanny's many old sayings was "Man can love the sea, but he must also respect it because he will never master it".*
Courtesy Mary Spaven.

possession. It must never be given away. If the caul is passed on, its protective magic goes to the person who has it". With equal resolve, Olive defended her action in giving it to a trawlerman who was at a greater risk of drowning than her daughter. The argument was not over the money — that was irrelevant —the anger was over the fact that Olive had given it away.

Husband Fred Harper was a gentle sort whose philosophy of life was 'peace at any price'. As he and his family lived in the house of his fiery mother-in-law he was keen to de-fuse the situation. He volunteered to teach 'Little Mary' to swim — thus lessening her chances of drowning. At regular intervals, he took her to Albert Avenue Baths. Within a short time, she was a good swimmer for her age. This was a logical move for Fred whose nickname was The Driffield Water Rat. As a young lad he saved a child from drowning in the River Head, the source of the Navigation Canal. The swimming lessons went someway to pacifying Grandma. But for years afterwards, whenever the topic of drowning came up, she never failed to hammer home the point that, "Mary's caul should never have left this family".

The above Wegg and Harper stories illustrate that the protective magic of the veil can transfer to whoever carries it. It is unique within the realm of superstition that this power can pass from one person to another.

One skipper carried a caul in a small seal-skin pouch on a leather thong around his neck. He was the only one of three sea-faring brothers born with a caul. The other two drowned at sea. Although a strong Roman Catholic, he firmly believed it was the caul which looked after him through his sea-going days. In some Hessle Road families the veil is stretched out on a piece of brown paper.

The ancient thinking about the protective value of the caul is convoluted. A caul protects the child before birth, so it will do so afterwards. Other attributes of the veil are that it gives the possessor skills in oratory and the gift of clairvoyance. Witches are reputed to put cauls in a cauldron when conjuring up magic spells.

When I tried to trace the origin of this superstition, it led into some colourful areas. Moses covered his radiant face with a veil after he had been in the presence of the Lord to receive the Ten Commandments (Exodus 34:33-35). And even the top of Mount Sinai was shrouded in a veil-like cloud during the forty days and forty nights he was up there (Exodus 24: 15-18). In Irish Mythology there is the tale of Moranni who became a judge and Druid in ancient Ulster. "He was born with a caul on his head and his father, judging him to be a monster, gave an order for him to be drowned at sea. Two servants went to perform the task and as he was dropped into the water a surge broke the helmet and the baby immediately spoke. The servants then rescued the boy and left him at the door of a smith. The smith raised him and eventually returned him to his father" (Ellis, 1987, p.172). So here is a story which links the caul with being saved from drowning. To the Romans the lucky caul was "a charm against death by drowning" (Brewer, 1990, p.209).

Common knowledge presumes that the caul protects the foetus from drowning while it grows in the watery womb. And, therefore, by mimic magic, the caul will do likewise for seafarers. Scientific evidence, however, shows that

24

"the foetus rests within a closed membrane (amniotic sac)...and this fluid-filled sac absorbs shock, equalises pressure...and provides nourishment" (Considine, 1989, p.1059). The caul, therefore, keeps water in — like a water-filled balloon — not out.

The value of the caul comes from its rarity. To the medical world, it is merely part of the discarded after-birth — so no records have been kept of how often babies are born with one. Nevertheless, we are talking about a probability of thousands-to-one. If that was the case in olden times, nowadays modern paediatric medicine reduces the chances of a caul-birth to zero. Midwife lecturer Gillian Brown recalls that when she did home deliveries in Hull's fishing community during the 1960s, there were about two or three cauls in her experience. But with induced hospital births, cauls are even less likely than with natural births at home. So yet another fragile cord with ancient superstition has been cut.

After the child was born, the Hessle Road mother found doors slammed in her face unless she performed two vital superstitious rituals.

## Chapter 3

### 'GOD'S HOUSE'

PROVERB: *Children are the anchors that
hold a mother to life.* (Greek)

Soon after the delivery of her child, a mother in the community — whether superstitious or not — was under strong social pressure to conform to two long-established rituals. Both these practices were common throughout Britain, but they were especially enforced in Hull's fishing community. The first of these was for the woman to get herself 'churched' — even if she was not a church-goer.

### CHURCHING

Some relatives, friends, and neighbours bluntly refused to let a new mum set foot in their home — or even speak to her in extreme cases — until she had been 'churched'. They were afraid of the bad luck she would bring. There is a Hessle Road saying, "Before you go into anyone else's house, you've got to go into God's House". Peter Nicholson, from the Hessle Road furniture shop, recalls chatting on the doorstep to one of his Gillett Street customers (c.1965), when a young woman came to call. Peter was taken aback by the rough manner the visitor was ordered away. He commented on this and was told, "She's just had a baby and ain't been churched yet!".

Being 'churched' was something a woman did alone — certainly not with her husband. Furthermore, it had nothing to do with the child. In some parts of the country a special blessing is performed by a vicar. But ministers prefer to see this as a 'Thanks giving' ceremony for both the child and the mother. More often than not, a Hessle Roader simply slipped in to sit at the back of the church or chapel toward the end of a regular service. There was no direct contact with the priest and he was unaware that a woman in his congregation was undertaking the 'churching' ritual. In an interview with Margaret and Brian Tate (who were active members of the Thornton Hall Methodist Mission on Hessle Road), I inquired if the fishing families were religious in any way. They said, "Generally, no" and explained that, "The fishing community had more like a superstitious religion. Right up to our Mission closing down [Jan. 1977], young mothers popped in to be 'churched'. The mother came in, perhaps just toward the end of the service — as soon as she was able to walk after the delivery. None of her relatives or friends let her into their houses until she had been churched. This was primarily a fisherfolk superstition, not a faith".

This last statement neatly sums up the dilemma which confronts the church — even today. A HDM headline recently read: 'Vicar Hits Out at Superstition'. A local priest claimed that 'churching' is unchristian, grossly insulting, sinister, dangerous and threatens to break up families (HDM, 5 Apr. 93, p.5). In St.

Peter's Anlaby (near Hull) Parish magazine, Reverend Francis Gordon-Kerr "launched his attack after hearing of a young mum who was turned away from her mother's home because she had not been 'churched'". He refused to perform any purification ceremony "which inferred that chldren and mothers were unclean until blessed". One week later the HDM printed a letter from Gil Reid, Boulevard, Hessle Road, which duly pointed out that the notion of 'unclean' originates from the Bible (Leviticus 12: 1-8). The mother "is unclean for 40 days after having a son and 80 days after a daughter...All in all the writers of the Bible had a very poor opinion of women" (HDM, 12 Apr. 93).

It sounds as if there is confusion within the Church about the whole business of 'churching'. It is not a practice they have initiated or encourage. Equally, the mothers themselves do not see giving birth as 'unclean'. This description has been imposed upon them by outsiders who rarely discuss the underlying reasons for this ancient ceremony. Giving birth is not unclean, indeed, it is a wholesome, pure process essential for the continuance of life.

I suspect that mothers have been getting 'churched' long before the Church came into being. The emotional state of pregnancy and conception is an uplifting experience. The mother goes through a heightened state (agony and ecstasy) at this critical life-and-death time. In this situation she is 'confined' not only to protect her from harmful spiritual forces, but also to insulate her from the community. The only way she can come down from her sacred contagious state is to undertake a ritual of return (to everyday life) — to come back down to earth — by a visit to a holy place. In Pagan times, this was probably a sacred spring in which she symbolically bathed. Thus, when the Hessle Roaders sent an unchurched mother from their doorstep, they re-enacted a long-forgotten primitive practice.

*BAPTISM*

The second social pressure on a mother can also be traced to pre-Christian times — but this ritual has been happily incorporated into the Church. That is, the urgency to get a child baptised at a font (a common practice throughout Britain until recent times). The idea is that the blessing by holy water gives the child's soul protection from the evil forces which lurk all around. During the vulnerable time betweem birth and baptism, the child was sometimes shielded from the Devil by placing a small amount of salt in the cot. Salt is an incorruptible substance which Satan apparently hates, and so keeps clear (Ch.22).

Another fear is that an unbaptised baby is at serious risk from the child-snatching fairies. In Mediæval times, if a child became grotesquely deformed and ugly, parents believed it had been changed by mischievous elves. These unfortunate children, probably mentally handicapped, were referred to as 'changelings'. The monstrous fairies had 'exchanged' a beautiful baby for one of their own disfigured goblins. In olden times, the accusation was made that a deformed child was the 'Wrath of God' upon sinful parents. "The poor fairies, therefore, were blamed" by the couple (Edwards, 1974, p.50).

Superstitions like these drove Hessle Roaders to get their newborn infants baptised as soon as possible. Church and chapel ministers were often asked,

*Above is a picture from the 1924 Baptism Certificate of St. Mary & St. Peter's Dairycoates Church on Hessle Road. The places of worship usually had set times when they conducted Christenings. But at the Fishermen's Bethel, Pastor Tom Chappell was flexible about when he performed the ceremony. Tom's regular days were Sundays and Tuesdays. One mother recalled that her trawling husband was due home on a Thursday morning tide and he wanted to see his son baptised. Tom, therefore, arranged a special service for that afternoon before the father sailed off the next day back to the Arctic waters.*
Courtesy Betty Dawson (she kindly donated this certificate for my research).

"Do you do babies?" — meaning a baptism. From 1875 to 1925, St. John the Baptist Church of Newington, christened 17,600 infants. The Fishermen's Bethel performed as many as 20,000 in less than thirty years from 1938 onwards. Indeed, the fishing families were perhaps closest to the non-denominational Bethel than to any other place of worship. Pastors there did not ask too many awkward questions about who the father was, or press families into regular attendance before and after the baptism.

In essence, a birth on Hessle Road was a period when Pagan ritual intermingled with Christian services during the crucial time when a newborn came into the world. Fishing families intuitively recognised the need for a rite of passage (return to routine) for the mother after her stressful experience. And the two major mechanisms whereby a mum was welcomed back into everyday life was by a quick visit to 'God's House' and later having the child baptised. Both were then 'safe' to mix with the rest of society.

Cordelia Jones (81) recalls, "When you met a new baby you always put a silver 6d. in its hand. This was good luck for both the child and yourself". In some families they gave salt and an egg. Salt symbolises "health in mind and body, and the egg signifies fertility and immortality" (Reader's Digest, 1977, p.50).

And so, from the instant of birth, the Hessle Road child was subjected to superstition which surrounded him or her for the rest of their lives.

## Chapter 4

## 'A WHISTLING WOMAN...'

*...and a crowing hen,*
*Bring the Devil out of his den'.*

Young Hessle Road girls were firmly told, "It is not lady-like to whistle". Indeed, as Edith Casey mentions, "a woman was considered 'common' if she whistled". Another version of the well-known proverb (used in the title of this chapter) is: "A whistling woman and a crowing hen is neither good for God nor men". The fear is that a woman has the ability to whistle up the wind and cause ships to sink at sea or be wrecked ashore.

The whistling taboo reflects, once again, the folklore belief in mimic magic. The human whistle sounds like the wind as it whistles and howls — a sound that haunts and disturbs mariners. The link between the wind and a whistling woman testifies to the fishermen's ancient fear of the witch (Ch. 33). It was once widely held that witches controlled the weather. Through sympathetic magic they influenced not just the wind, but also rain, storms, thunder, and lightning.

In 1592 around a dozen witches were burnt to death accused of causing shipwrecks along the coast of North Berwick. A more recent incident and one closer to Hull was described by Anson (1932). He tells how Yorkshire wives of fishermen, in 1886, performed a midnight ritual to exorcise their men's unlucky boats (p.83). In some primitive cultures, a woman was not allowed to touch or step over the fishing nets — especially if she was pregnant or menstruating —they would be cursed. The only remedy was to burn the nets straight away. At the mystical level, all women are potential witches. Therefore, the actions of the men's wives and daughters were restricted by a complex web of rituals which limited the women's actions while the trawlermen were away.

The whistling taboo also affected the men at sea. Wireless operator and musician Ron Haines loved to whistle. But when he first went to sea in January 1940 he was soon told off. Crewmen warned, "You'll whistle up the wind". Former trawlerman Ray Hotham — now an attendant on the Spurn Light-ship in the Hull Marina — relates the expression: 'Soldiers whistle; Sailors sing'.

Jerome Willis (1937) described a situation in which Hull trawlermen believed whistlng at sea was to their financial advantage. In his book *The Last Adventurers* he told of the return of the *Bayflower* (H.487) from the deep-sea grounds with its fish rooms full to the hatches. Strangely, the crew whistled loudly as their trawler battled in a raging North Sea storm. On the bridge, during the late-night watch, even skipper Big Chris joined in the whistling chorus. The men's motive was to keep the North Sea in a violent mood so that east-coast fishermen would be unable to catch or land any fish at Bridlington or Scarborough. They hoped that when the *Bayflower* sold its prime catch, it would fetch handsome settlings. So the men merrily whistled away in the sure belief that this old wives' tale was true (p.61).

Back ashore, Freda Fee remembers that net braiders "were not allowed to whistle at work". Once, when they were all put on short time, they blamed a woman who happened to whistle.

This whole section, about the supernatural power of the female, is best concluded by giving the last word to a woman. At the end of my talk about superstitions to the retired staff of Ideal Standard (10/91), Olive Westcott gave me an extended version of the old proverb. It goes like this:

> *"A Whistling Woman and Crowing Hen*
> *May bring the Devil out of his Den;*
> *But the Woman who whistles*
> *And the Hen that Doth Crow*
> *Go far in Life*
> *wherever they go."*

*It was not uncommon for Hessle Road children to be brought up by their grandparents. Many youngsters lost their father – either at sea or during wartime. This is Laura Brown with her children: Cordelia (left), Ivy and newly-born Charles. Their father, Henry, died in France in 1917. Young Cordelia absorbed many of Grandma Taylor's folk beliefs; and kindly re-told many of them during my research. I love to listen to her tales of the olden days.*
Courtesy Marion Toffolo.

31

**Chapter 5**

## EVIL EYE and ITCHY FEET
SAYING: *If looks could kill.*

Our own bodies attract various folklore beliefs. Specific parts of the anatomy, mentioned during many interviews, included the eyes, hair, nails, fingers, feet, and itching sensations.

The most powerful of these taboos was the 'Evil Eye'. For nearly fifty years Charles Ayre ferried crewmen out to waiting trawlers in the Humber. One passenger, a skipper, always cursed a lady in his street as "Mrs. So-and-So, that squint-eyed old woman". If ever this skipper met any cross-eyed woman when going out to place a bet, he turned around, went back home and refused to gamble that day for he was sure to lose. Olive Fisher. who worked at Cloggie Walsh's Clog Shop on Hessle Road, points out that, "It was unlucky to meet a cross-eyed woman, but a cross-eyed man was a lucky sign". After a thoughtful pause Olive added, "I believe in Demons — and you have got to be careful when you talk about them",

The *Encyclopædia of Magic and Superstition* outlined a long string of dire consequence: "The immediate effect of a blast from the Evil Eye upon a victim involves not only misfortunes of every kind, but inflictions of the worst diseases, often leading to death. The sexual organs were particularly liable to psychic assaults...impotence and frigidity...minor disorders such as headaches and hiccups were common signs of having been overlooked". The text added that "The pig was the one animal who was extremely vulnerable to the effects of the Evil Eye" (Blackcat, 1988, p.83).

From the eyes, we move upwards to the hair. As far as superstitions are concerned, the cutting of hair and finger-nails can be paired together. The common expression is that: "To cut hair or nails at sea will provoke a storm. And to cut nails on a Sunday means that you will have the Devil with you all the week". According to Frazer (1922) "Superstitions related to hair and nail cutting are world wide" (p.38). He cited a Roman maxim that, "No one on shipboard should cut his hair or nails except in a storm. That is, when the mischief was already done...In the Highlands of Scotland it was said that no sister should comb her hair at night if she has a brother at sea" (p.234).

The ancient belief is that hair, because it is associated with the head, has magical properties of its own. This point is well illustrated by the Bible. Samson lost his physical strength after his hair had been cut off by Delilah (Judges 16:9). And, even today, prisoners of war are humiliated by having their hair shaved off (in former Yugoslavia), especially if of Islamic faith. In Black Magic an evil spell cannot work unless something of the victim is used to form a potent link. Hair and small nail pairings are ideal in casting spells. This is why primitive tribes have protective rituals when hair is being cut.

One woman told how her father firmly forbade anyone in his family from cutting nails on a Friday. This trawler bosun believed that to do this was "to *nail* Christ to the cross again". This is a curious application of sympathetic magic in that Friday is linked with the crucifixion on Good Friday, and finger nails are associated with the iron nails hammered through His limbs. "Keeping your fingers crossed" is a common way to ward off bad luck. This too symbolises the cross of Christ. A Christian belief attached to this superstition is that with two fingers crossed, that leaves the thumb and two other fingers to symbolise the Trinity — for further protection against evil.

The half-moons and white spots found on finger nails were a childhood game to foretell future events. Also in childhood, youngsters were often told, "It's rude to point" — and it is especially dangerous to point at a ship — for fear that it will sink at sea. Instead, the whole hand is used.

An assistant in a Hessle Road toy shop always told children, "Do not swing your feet, it's unlucky". But, as with most of these dire warnings, no explanation was given as to 'Why'. I have yet to come across an answer to this in the literature. But it sounds similar to the warning, "Not to swing on doors". The thinking here being that the draught will cause a storm at sea for the fishing boats.

Clara Magee (89) mentioned that if your ears burn, then someone was talking about you. "Left for love, Right for spite". She also mentioned itches in different parts of the body which foretold future events. Shortly after this interview, I came across a fairly full list of what itching means in John Nicholson's (1890) book, *Folk Lore of East Yorkshire*. An itch in the right eye means a surprise awaits; the left eye means you will soon cry. Should your nose itch you will soon be angry. An itchy right palm predicts the reception of money; and the left indicates you will soon be paying out — "right to receive, left to leave". An itch in the right foot means you will step on strange ground (travel in store) and on the left foot? — Nicholson did not say (p.44).

# PART TWO
## FOLK (AFLOAT):
### Men at Sea

## Chapter 6
### MEN ONLY

PROVERB: *Time and Tide wait for no man.*

Women are allowed aboard trawlers from countries like Iceland, Germany, and Russia — and work very hard too. But as far as Hull trawlermen are concerned, women are taboo. This is a long-held anti-women superstition. She is feared as a sort of Jonah.

But, as with all prohibitions, there are exceptions to the rule. And not everyone took notice of the ill omens. So far, I have heard of three cases whereby a woman was sneaked on board and taken to the deep-sea grounds —obviously there are other examples and I am always keen to hear about them. The outcome of these three voyages was not as disastrous as folklore would have us believe —except perhaps for the first tale.

In the 1930s, a North Shields prostitute was smuggled aboard a Newington Steam Fishing trawler (perhaps the *Conan Doyle* — H.240) during an extended Hull party. It is believed that the skipper, who shall remain nameless, was involved in this caper. The story goes that she fell asleep and did not wake until the ship was well out into the North Sea. Her reaction was, "Well, no one will miss me". And so she stayed for the whole voyage. There are few details, but it was said to be the worst-ever trip any of the crew experienced — details are sketchy.

In the second incident, trawlerman Stan Fairbrass remembers a woman coming aboard the *Nab Wyke* (H.252) in 1933 when he was a fresh young deckie-learner. The trawler had just left St. Andrew's Dock and was steaming off the Minerva Pier when the pilot boat came alongside with an unusual passenger. It was skipper Charlie Whiting's wife who slipped aboard the 140ft trawler. Stan describes her as "a nice woman" who stayed in the skipper's cabin unless the weather was fine. Young Stan had the job of taking her a cup of tea and sandwich. At the end of the three-week trip Charlie called up his pilot pals. They took his wife off the 1930-built vessel. Thus, she was not seen by the owners West Dock Steam Fishing. After being landed at the pier, she may well have got a taxi to St. Andrew's Dock to pick up her husband. No doubt the Whitings had a good laugh at defying the rules of the fishing industry and at disproving the deep-seated non-woman taboo. Stan could not recall the trip being an unlucky one. This *Nab Wyke* example is one which proved the superstition wrong. There is one more similar tale of a skipper taking his wife to sea. But this was not out of choice or defiance. Nevertheless, he was punished by the owners.

Top skipper Harold Hall told his own story in the *Hull Daily Mail – Fishing Years* supplement (No.1, 9 Apr. 88, p.20) and I subsequently interviewed him (6/93). He was just about to set off on a trip when his wife Annie felt depressed (c.1960). The family doctor told him not to leave his wife alone. Harold was in a cleft stick. It was far too late to find a replacement skipper; and he could not abandon Annie. He decided there was only one thing to do — sneak her aboard

*Chief engineer Terence Musgreaves adamantly believed it was very dangerous
to return home once having set foot outdoors. During the 1950s he sailed
regularly aboard the Hudson trawlers. But on one trip there were serious problems
with the engines – so the sailing orders were cancelled.
This placed Terry in a difficult dilemma. He dared not return home to his
Preston Road prefab. Instead, he spent the night at a friend's house to prevent
bringing bad luck upon his family.*
Courtesy Bonita Musgreaves.

the *Lord Willoughby* (H.36). By looking after her there, he thus complied with
the doctor's orders. Harold said he is not superstitious at all. He was born on the
13 December 1913 and he sees that number as being lucky for him.

It was a good voyage worth about £10,000, and the trip did Annie "the world
of good". Indeed, while at the grounds she pleased the crew by handing them
tots of whiskey through the chart-room porthole — but Harold was none too
pleased. After they returned to St. Andrew's Dock, he sneaked Annie into a taxi
and they went home. The skipper left orders with the mate to sign up ALL the
same crew and not dismiss anyone. But for some reason he sacked two
sparehands. Out of malice they reported to owner Tom Boyd that Skipper Hall
had taken his wife to sea. Harold was summoned to see The Gaffer to explain
what had happened. Although sympathetic with Harold's plight, Boyd
nevertheless had to suspend him. Normally, it would have been a three-month
'walkabout', but as Harold was one of the company's top-earners, it was
reduced to one trip only. This token punishment was to demonstrate that
Harold had broken one of the industry's unwritten rules — a disguised
superstition which meant that Hull trawlers were for 'men only'.

# Chapter 7

## 'DON'T TURN BACK'

SHAKESPEARE: *There is a tide in the affairs of men*
*Which, taken at the flood, leads on to fortune;*
*Omitted, all the voyage of their life*
*Is bound in shallows and in miseries.*
*On such a full sea are we now afloat.*
(Julius Caesar)

From the raw deckie-learner to the tough skipper (and including the trawler owners themselves) superstition swam through the industry like fish in the seas. Hull's distant-water trawlermen followed the ancient taboos handed to them from the days of sail when the Brixham smackmen founded the port's fishing industry. Many crewmen were unconsciously on the look out for hidden omens from the start to the finish of a trawling trip. Indeed, from the moment some packed their sea bag.

Fred Casey, who sailed mainly with the Marr fleet after the Second World War, "was deadly serious over superstitions". One of his strongest taboos, which still causes a chuckle in the Casey family, revolved around the packing of his sea-bag. Once something was placed inside, "You were NOT allowed to take it out again. Otherwise, he'd not go to sea". Fred and his wife Edith had six lively youngsters. They have happy childhood memories of dad's sea-bag and its contents. Whenever Fred returned after a three-week trip he always treated his family to an extra large 7lb. box of Quality Street chocolates. Edie recalls that when Fred arrived home at No. 17 Harrow Street, "the kids eagerly waited to dive into his bag". And when the chocolates appeared "they made a feast of 'em".

Fred's sea-bag was part of the family fun. When the time came for dad to set off again — he was always anxious to get down on dock about two hours before sailing time — his children were keen to give mam a hand in packing. Toys, inevitably, got dropped into his bag. On rare occasions, if she knew Fred had not seem them go in, she secretly sneaked the items out again. At the start of many a trip, Fred set off with his sea-bag full of useless junk.

Another sea-bag taboo was that a trawlerman must never lift it on his shoulder whilst indoors. This constraint seems to parallel the popular belief about "Not putting an umbrella up in the house" (a superstition, incidentally, never mentioned by any Hessle Roader during my interviews — perhaps because umbrellas were not too common in the community?). Once the man was outdoors it was safe to place the sea-bag on his shoulder.

What is fascinating about this research was coming across highly specific superstitions which were peculiar to an individual family — as opposed to the widespread beliefs. This was illustrated in bosun Thomas Palmer Jones' home

*Fred Casey in 1954 having a dram in St. Andrew's Club (West Dock Avenue) with his eldest son Norman – who had just turned 18-years of age – old enough to drink. One of Fred's many superstitions was never to take anything out of his sea bag once it had been placed inside. Consequently, after his children helped mam pack his bag, Fred often took a load of junk off to sea with him.*
Courtesy Edith Casey.

at No. 46 Eton Street. He was "superstitious, but didn't make a thing of it", recalls his daughter Edna Clarke. Tom sailed for years with his best friend, George Double — 'one of the luckiest skippers out of Hull' during the 1920s aboard the *St. Leander* (H.420). Whenever Tom set off on a trawling trip, it was little Edna's dutiful game to throw dad's slipper down the passage at the front door. This was "to ensure that he'd come back safely to wear them again". I do not know the exact origin of this slipper-throwing superstition, but I have read that in some British ports there was a tradition whereby an old boot was thrown after a fishing boat as it left the harbour — to wish a good trip for those on board (Rhea, 1985, p.25). And, of course, it is widely known that old boots are tied behind a wedding car as a good luck token for the happy couple. "The shoe has long been a symbol of female sexuality...an ancient way of wishing fertility on the marriage" (Reader's Digest, 1977, p.55) — thus the rhyme: "There was an old woman who lived in a shoe / She had so many children, she didn't know what to do". The fishing equivalent, no doubt, is to wish a trawlermen a fruitful trip.

*Happier days for Skipper Parkes of the **Endon** (H.161) playing the accordion and smoking his pipe (c.1932). On his right is banjo-playing Victor Harbord. Can anyone name any other members of this musical crew? Prior to the **Endon's** ill-omened Christmas trip in 1932, Victor morbidly told his wife, "If anything happens to me, I hope you get my body back".*

*Lilian Gladys Harbord was the only **Endon** widow to have her husband's body returned from the sea. The photograph below shows her in black attending the Coroner's Court. She startled the inquest when she declared that the body of the **Endon's** deckie-learner had been found by the **Stronsay** (H.387). But the frightened crew flung it back into the North Sea because of the strong belief against having a corpse on board.*      Courtesy Victor Harbord Snr.

Many crewmen had a taxi waiting outside their house to take them to St. Andrew's Fish Dock, especially a skipper. They usually had the same driver every time they came ashore. Each driver knew when a regular customer was due to land by reading the Russell's list — a sheet printed each week for the fish merchants stating how much fish was aboard each trawler and on which tide she was due to dock. The 'sticking with the same' driver ritual can be seen as a disguised superstition — for to change the taxi may change one's luck. Once at the dockside, some skippers had a strong belief that he must never get on board (or off) carrying his own sea-bag — a job usually done by the cabbie. Conversely, school lads sometimes hung around the fish dock at tide time to carry men's bags on board — knowing that they were in line for a handsome tip for this small favour. And so, unwittingly, a few bob was made out of this old superstition. An elderly trawlerman mentioned that once the vessel steamed into the Humber, "the crew never looked back at the fish dock gates — only forward to the open waters ahead".

Once at sea it was considered very unlucky if the trawler turned back or had a 'broken trip'. The mysterious loss of the *Endon* (H.161) is cited as an example of how this superstition invoked a dire premonition. In December 1932 her bosun Victor Harbord (31), unexpectedly returned home to No. 2 Seaton Grove, Gipsyville. The *Endon* had been at sea only a week when forced to return after Mate Richards was lost overboard. Victor gravely told his wife Lilian, "If anything happens to me, I hope you get my body back". He also persuaded the young deckie-learner William Crecy (16) to get deck experience aboard the *Grouse* (H.193). The lad took this advice and lived; but something strange happened to his replacement on the *Endon* — Harry Anderson. Second engineer Edward Holmes of No. 69 Somerset Street was also highly disturbed by the return of his trawler and bleakly told his daughter, "The *Endon* will be my coffin". This 1914-built ship was part of the rapidly declining Red Cross boxing fleet which trawled the depleted North Sea grounds. With a new mate, deckie-learner, and disturbed crew, the *Endon* set sail for her Christmas trip under the command of Skipper Parkes.

The mystery began when the Hull trawler *St. Kilda* (H.355) spotted the *Endon* adrift — eerily, she had all her fishing gear down and deck lights ablaze. Skipper William Rutland sent three men over to the helpless vessel. To their amazement, there was not a soul on board the 235-ton trawler. All ten crewmen had vanished into thin air. What they found was that the *Endon* had a seven-foot gash along her side and that the lifeboat had gone. It looked as if she had been in a collision and that the crew had hastily, yet needlessly, abandoned ship. No other collision vessel was ever traced. Under these strange circumstances, all the *St. Kilda* could do was take the abandoned vessel in tow with the intention of bringing her home to Hull. It was not to be. Rough weather made this task extremely difficult. When it looked as if the distressed vessel was going to sink, Rutland released her to the elements. For the second time the *Endon* deceived crewmen into thinking she was doomed.

Strange and spooky tales of the *Endon* spread throughout the community soon after the *St. Kilda* steamed into St. Andrew's Dock with her flag at half mast. This morbid signal always caused a stir and work stopped momentarily on the busy fish dock. Out of respect, and superstition, the crew waited while a corpse was carried ashore.

It was the body of bosun Victor Harbord. His life-belted body had subsequently been found by the *St. Kilda* floating in the vicinity of the *Endon*. The pastor of the Fishermen's Bethel was notified and he immediately set off to 'break the news' to Lilian Harbord — but she was not at home. She was described as "one of the most popular women on the Gipsyville housing estate". The Harbord's (originally from Lowestoft) had a boy (12) and girl (5). That afternoon, Lilian had "gathered together half-a-dozen children playing about on the street and, with her own youngsters, took them to the Langham" — a large newly-opened cinema on Hessle Road — to see the afternoon matinée. The excited group joked in the foyer when Pastor Joseph 'Pop' Summers found the laughing group. He took Lilian aside and quietly told her about the loss of the *Endon* and that Victor's body was the only one found. "She was dazed and silenced", and her first wish was to see the corpse. No doubt she recalled Victor's morbid foreboding about her getting his body back.

Meanwhile, the crew of the *Stronsay* (H.387) trawled up the body of the *Endon's* new deckie-learner Anderson. But they threw it back into the North Sea because it was unlucky to have a corpse aboard a Hull trawler. Lilian Harbord made this known to the Hull Coroner after she spoke to the *Stronsay's* trimmer. The lad's body was "thrown back after being recognised as they did not want a dead man on board" (HDM 10 Jan. 33).

Even a full week after the *St. Kilda* had released the *Endon*, other Hull trawlers reported having seen the uncanny vessel adrift in the choppy North Sea. Like a ghost ship she roamed aimless and soul-less. In some quarters, the *Endon* was dubbed the *Marie Celeste* — because of the weird absence of the crewmen from a ship not in danger of immediately sinking. Others took a more modernistic view. They speculated that their loved ones had been seized by Men from Mars in a Flying Saucer — rumours fuelled by popular science-fiction stories of that time like H. G. Wells' *War of the Worlds*.

The strong theme which ran through most of these leaving-home superstitions was to 'never turn back once embarking upon a trawling (hunting) trip. In other words, keep going forward, regardless. But, as we will see, even this strong taboo could be over-ruled by an even stronger animal superstition (Ch. 18).

*Victor Harbord was laid to rest in Hull's Northern Cemetery. His family wanted to ensure that his crewmates were also not forgotten. So the grave was incribed: "In Memory of the Crew of s.t. **Endon** – Lost at sea". Grandson Victor, who occasionally visits the grave, was shocked when he found that the authorities had smashed up the sole memorial of this trawling tragedy (along with adjacent monuments c.1971). After complaining, the original wording was put back on a replacement head-stone (right).*
*Courtesy Victor Harbord Snr.*

IN LOVING MEMORY OF
MY DEAR HUSBAND
VICTOR E. HARBORD
DROWNED OFF S.T. "ENDON"
JAN. 3RD 1933, AGED 31.
HIS LOVING HANDS WILL TOIL NO MORE
ALSO THE CREW OF S.T. "ENDON"
LOST AT SEA.
ALSO HIS SON
VICTOR EDWARD
DIED NOV. 23RD 1971, AGED 51.
A LOVING HUSBAND & FATHER.
ALSO A DEAR WIFE
AND MOTHER OF THE ABOVE
LILLIAN GLADYS JOLLEY
DIED OCT. 23RD 1974, AGED 7

## Chapter 8

## TRAGIC and MAGIC NAMES

PROVERB: *He who is not lucky,*
*Let him not go to sea. (*Latin)

The original name of a ship is sacrosanct. It is steeped in magic, and a trawler is unlucky if it is re-named. Chief engineer Frank Wilson of No. 118 Flinton Street had more than enough reason to believe this taboo.

Shortly after the Second World War his newly-married son Ron (21), whose wife Edna was expecting their first child, had just been demobbed. His war service had been aboard Merchant Navy 'big boats'. Ron was keen to follow in his father's wake and got himself a coal-trimming job aboard the *Kingston Pearl* (H.542) bound for the Norwegian fishing grounds in January 1946. The Kingston class of trawlers had already been unlucky for the Wilson family. Frank's son-in-law Charles Bateson was aboard the *Kingston Ceylonite* (H.173) when she was blown in half (off Chesapeake Bay, Virginia, in the Atlantic) on 15 June 1942. This Beverley-built trawler was on loan by the British Admiralty to the U. S. Navy who were laying and sweeping when she blew up amidships. It was a miracle that Charlie lived. He was in a U. S. Naval Hospital for three years as they re-built his face with wires, and made him a set of special teeth.

But it was not the fact that Frank's own son Ron had joined a Kingston vessel. It was something else about its name which disturbed him. The *Kingston Pearl* had recently had her name changed from the *Scottish* (GY.397) — it was this 'change' aspect which made him fearful. Bad luck struck the *Pearl* as she steamed homeward on the 16 February. A giant wave hit her starboard beam. The 558-ton vessel suddenly heeled to port and the wheelhouse was swamped. The funnel bent nearly into the engine-room casing. The engine-room itself was flooded and Ron was thrown across the stoke hold. He was hurled into a piece of protruding machinery which punctured his stomach. Still conscious, he managed to stagger unaided onto the mess deck. No one fully realised at that time that he was in such a bad way. Ron was merely treated with a Solution of Iodine. His brave fight for life ended in the early hours of 19 February as the *Pearl* slowly struggled back to Hull. The shock to the Wilson family was so great that Ron's mother Ada was "never the same again". And Frank's anxiety that a trawler's name must never be changed stayed with him until the end.

Nevertheless, despite this pervading taboo, Hull trawler names were regularly changed at an alarming rate. During my survey of nearly 3000 vessels for (900) *Lost Trawlers of Hull*, I found names changed frequently as vessels went from company to company. Hull firms use evocative thematic names for their trawlers such as the Charleson-Smith *Stella* fleet named after various star constellations (*Stella Antares* — H.123). Thomas Hamling used mythical saints (*St. Amandus* — H.247). The powerful Hellyer family had two major fleets.

42

One named after Shakespearian characters (*Othello* — H.581) and another after historic tribes (*Kelt* — H.193). Therefore, when a particular firm purchased a second-hand trawler, its name was invariably changed to harmonize with their established fleet series. This was illustrated on a grand scale in the 1960s when the Ross Group bought up various small trawler firms and re-named all their acquisitions with the *Ross* prefix (*Cape Trafalgar* — H.59 became the *Ross Trafalgar*). Furthermore, when the British Admiralty requisitioned Hull's best trawlers before and during both world wars, they also tended to change names according to their classification system. Hull's *Lady Lilian* (H.467), for example, became the H.M.T. *Jade* (T.56) — this was the Navy's 'Gem' class — she was lost 22 April 1942 when bombed by aircraft in Malta's Grand Harbour.

*James Ronald Wilson – known simply as Ron – died three days after a giant wave hit the* **Kingston Pearl** *(H.542) on 16 February 1946. This was his very first trawling trip shortly after being demobbed from war service in the Royal Navy. His father Frank was fearful of him going on this trawler because it had recently had a name change. In the world of superstition it is unlucky to change anything as sacrosanct as a ship's original name.*
Courtesy Marian Chambers

In essence, name change was not uncommon for the trawlers. But whenever disaster struck, the fact that a name change had taken place did not go without mention. But what often got overlooked were all the name-changed trawlers which did not sink or get into serious difficulties.

One frequently cited example of a lost trawler is the *Roderigo* (H.135 — obviously a Hellyer vessel). Along with the *Lorella* (H.455) she iced-up and sank off the north-west coast of Iceland in January 1955. The *Roderigo* had previously been the *Princess Elizabeth* owned by Boston Deep-Sea Fisheries (the Parkes family). A 'superstitious study' of this 810-ton side-winder reveals a history of ominous events. After being built in 1950 at Beverley, she failed to enter the River Hull at the first launch. And even during her trials in the Humber "everything went wrong and she ran aground at Paull". Her maiden voyage was cursed too. She only got as far as Spurn, took a sea badly and returned home water-logged. When she got to the fishing grounds "she was like a dead thing and just wouldn't fish". Steaming home, second engineer Will Price died of double pneumonia "the crew didn't like walking past the room" where he was laid out (W. Mimms, *Fishing Years*, No. 4, May 90, p.15). Soon afterwards, Boston Deep-Sea Fisheries sold this 'bad sea ship' to Hellyers and she was re-named *Roderigo* — a doomed vessel.

On the humorous side, there is another story which centres upon the significance of a trawler's name. It is told by Terry Robins, a retired director of West Dock Steam Fishing Company. This company's thematic naming pattern was to suffix their vessels with the word *Wyke* (which is the ancient name for Hull) e.g., *Staxton Wyke* (H.479). In 1922 they purchased two ex-Admiralty WWI minesweepers. They named one of these *Cloughton Wyke* (H.705). The Robins placed her in the hands of their top skipper. He was 'over the moon' to be in command and was rather pleased with himself as he announced to the owners that he could make out the word "L-U-C-K" from her name. Terry Robins added with a twinkle, "But Uncle Wilf didn't have the heart to tell this chap that it was also possible to make out the words "NO LUCK" from her name!" The trawler owners themselves, however, were not above superstition when it came to ships' names. Hull's two surviving trawler-owning families still display examples of this — even in the 1990s.

First of all J. Marr & Sons whose recurring finger-print is to end their vessels' names with ...*ella* like *Swanella* (H.141). If a particular ship is lucky for them, they retain its name time and time again. The name *Northella*, for example, has been passed on from 1946 to five subsequent vessels [a practice very confusing for local historians, I must add]: 1946 = H.244; 1951 = H.159; 1958 = H.98; 1964 = H.301; and 1973 = H.206. Whereas the unlucky *Lorella*, lost with its 20-man crew in 1955, has never had her name repeated.

The other surviving Hull trawler firm has also shown that they are susceptible to the old naming tradition which pervades the industry. Boyd Line Limited (established in 1936) use their famous prefix *Arctic* .... followed by a swash-buckling pirate-type name like *Arctic Buccaneer* (H.188). In the financially gloomy post-Cod War period of the early 1980s, Boyd's bread-winning, record-breaking trawler was the *Arctic Corsair* (H.320). The feeling is that she was a successful and lucky ship for the company — and "won a special place in our hearts" says trawler manager Terry Thresh. So when she outlived her fishing days there was a reluctance to let go of her magic name. The surprise was that not only was the *Arctic Corsair's* name carried over to the modern freezer which Boyd bought in 1988, but also her H.320 Hull registration number was transferred to this new ship. It is a highly unusual practice to transfer both name and number from one vessel to another. The old 1960 side-winder *Corsair* was renamed *Arctic Cavalier*. Hopefully, she will become a central attraction in Hull's long-overdue tribute to the port's trawling heritage at the former St. Andrew's Fish Dock — but that is for the future.

There are yet further taboos associated with the way trawler names are spelt. There are some curious points in this regard. First, it is said that any ship beginning with the letter 'S' is unlucky. For those trawlermen who believed this taboo there were many problems. It means that literally scores of *Saint* trawlers which sailed from Hull were supposedly unlucky — though this is blatantly not the case. Linked with this 'S'-in-the-name superstition is the letter 'A'. There is a general maritime belief that any vessel whose name ends in 'A' is unlucky. The 'evidence' cited to support this belief is the loss of the ocean liner *Lusitania* on 7 May 1915 (Haining, 1979, p.151). Again, this taboo causes problems in Hull. All the Marr trawlers, for example, end with ...*ella*.

One can only conjecture why it should be that ship's beginning with the letter

'S' or ending in 'A' are unlucky. For what it is worth, my guess focuses upon the word 'SEA' which obviously begins with 'S' and ends with 'A'. If we support the ancient belief in the Spirits of the Sea, then it is not hard to accept that the sea would wish to claim anything like a ship or seaman whose name is similar to its own. This view is not too far fetched for anyone absorbed in folk mythology.

Superstitious bosun George Allan expressed the view that anyone with the letter 'S' in their name is in danger at sea. For years I heard hints about this specific letter taboo; but it was not until I met the Williams family — and they related their threefold tragedy — that I had a substantial story connected with this 'S'-in-the-name taboo. Their anguish began aboard the Hull-based trawler *Boston Lincoln* (GY.1399).

The dreadful incident happened on 30 January 1974 at the White Sea grounds. Aboard were two of the five Williams brothers from an old seafaring family. They were all trawlermen apart from the eldest Dave: "I only got as far as the lockpit [on a pleasure trip with his dad]. I jumped off and came home". The other four each suffered at sea in one way or another. But it was with Terry and Harry that the real tragic tale began off the Russian coast.

Both men left good trawlers after being personally asked to join the *Boston Lincoln* by her skipper. Stan Taylor was a friend who wanted to build up his own crew and knew "the two Williams lads were good grafters". Harry's wife Maureen told him, "You're a fool to go and leave a good ship you enjoy" [*Cordella* — H.177]. But it was out of loyalty, a bond of friendship with Stan, that both brothers joined his crew. By doing so, they broke another taboo. Besides the cursed 'S' in their surname, "it is unlucky for two relatives to sail together (as seamen) in the same vessel, as one of them will certainly be drowned" (Opie & Tatem, 1989, p.34).

The *Lincoln's* portside pin on the trawl gear kept jamming. The usual routine was for a deckhand to grab a spanner and bash it free. Terry was doing this when the cable suddenly freed, it caught him across the shoulder, whipped him over the bulwark, and he dropped unconscious on to the steep ramp at the stern of the ship. As his body slowly slid toward the icy water, his younger brother Harry — the junior bosun — leapt from the starboard side down onto the slippery ramp in a brave attempt to save Terry.

In pitch blackness (7.10 p.m.) crewmen called out, "Can you see the lifebelt?". Harry grabbed hold of it for a while, then seemed to let go as if to swim toward Terry. Although the *Lincoln* was only doing one knot, the two men soon disappeared from the rays of the ship's lights and were never seen again. It took about three minutes for the 846-ton freezer to turn around — but neither brother was found. Both men wore 'doffers' (thick duffle-type coats) and heavy thigh boots — the sea temperature was 28°F.

All the crew were depressed by this double death and were not happy to work. Boston Deep-Sea Fisheries agreed to bring the stern-loader home after only 16 days of a 16-week trip. Her flag was at half-mast as she steamed into St. Andrew's Dock. The 25-man crew joined over one hundred mourners at the Memorial Service for the Williams brothers at the RNMDSF's chapel in Goulton Street (on Bank), led by Supt. David Saltiel (c. 11 Feb. 1974). The *Boston Lincoln* sailed the next morning. In her empty fish room were the flowers

*The Williams brothers Terry and Harry were inseperable – even in death. They grew up together, went to sea together, took holidays together, drowned together, were miraculously both washed ashore in Soviet Russia, and eventually were brought back to Hull where they are now buried alongside each other. The above print shows Harry (left) and Terry at the Butlin's Holiday Camp, Filey, with their wives Maureen and Jean respectively.*
*Below (back row) are Terry and Harry as young deckie-learners with two of their pals (unnamed – July 1955). Whenever any of the four Williams brothers set off on a trawling trip, their mother Hilda often played 'Red Sails in the Sunset' by The Platters before they left home.*
Courtesy Maureen Williams.

from the service. These were cast into the White Sea at the place where Terry and Harry both drowned.

Meanwhile, news coverage of the Williams' tragedy was overshadowed by the horrific disappearance of the *Gaul* (H.243) with 36 men aboard (8 February 1974). Mystery immediately surrounded this modern super-trawler. She went suddenly, there was no distress signal or trace of any wreckage, and no bodies were found. Media headlines speculated that she was a 'spyship' and the Soviets were accused of being the prime culprits. The Russians still strenuously deny any involvement. When the Soviets found the body of an unidentified British fisherman near Murmansk, they automatically assumed it was from the *Gaul*. As a way of showing their innocence, they seemed to declare, "Look! Here's a body...we have nothing to hide". But the corpse was that of Terry Williams from the *Boston Lincoln* — photographs were sent to England and he was identified by his tattoos.

Although Terry's father was not bothered, eldest son Dave and Terry's widow wanted him home. And so a long campaign began. During endless correspondence (and Harold Wilson's personal involvement) it was revealed that there was another washed-ashore body. Miraculously, it was that of Harry (also identified by his tattoos). The edgy Soviet naval commanders made an unprecendented concession to let a Boston Fisheries trawler dock at their highly-secret naval base at Murmansk to collect the two Williams brothers.

This was a tremendous break through for the Williams family. But superstition stepped in to prevent the collection happening. Hull trawler crews refuse to sail with a corpse on board as we saw with the *Endon* (Ch.7). The once-in-a-life-time offer was rejected. Instead, the two exhumed bodies travelled overland by train to Leningrad. There, the British cable-laying ship *Lindisfarne* picked up the Williams brothers and landed them at Immingham. Robinson Funeral Directors on Hessle Road collected them by hearse and brought them home for burial. As Dave Williams walked away from the funeral parlour carrying the two bags of belongings of Terry and Harry, he had in his head the words of the Tom Jones song *The Green, Green Grass of Home* (Apr. 1975).

All in all, it took Dave two arduous years to help sort out both his sisters-in-law's legal claims for compensation. Then, on the very last day when Harry's business was finally settled, a third disaster struck another of the Williams family at the White Sea fishing grounds. Brother Brian was killed aboard the *St. Benedict* (H.164) on 25 May 1976. His most feared superstition revolved around birds — as we will see later (Ch.16).

The power of individual letters and of full words is further illustrated by a string of taboo words which must never be uttered aboard fishing boats. It seems that different ports around the country (and world) have different clusters of 'forbidden' words. The Hull-taboo words, drawn from the Mary Spaven (1984) list, reads "Knife, Pig, Hare, Cat, Egg, Dog, Church, Chapel, Manse". We are going to have fun in Part Three looking at the animals, Knife and Egg are examined as inanimate objects (Part Four), but the three religious words are considered next.

# Chapter 9

## TABOO WORDS

PROVERB: *No mischief but a woman or a priest*
*is at the bottom of it.* (Latin)

It is noteworthy that Hull trawlermen have an aversion to the uttering of Christian words such as 'Church' 'Chapel' and 'Manse'. These are a curious combination and provide a fascinating insight into the superstitious beliefs of the fishing families. The general feeling is that it is "unlucky to meet a clergyman on the way to the fish dock or to see one stood near a trawler". The origin of this anti-church view pre-dates Hull's fishing history.

A similar practice was reported as long ago as the 12th century. The Bishop of Exeter penalised his parishioners who adhered to the old belief that it was "unlucky to meet a priest". Eight hundred years later, this same folk fear was still strong. Radford (1974) described what happened between the ministers at a Methodist Conference and West Cornwall youngsters during the 1930s: "a strong protest was made concerning the disrespectful behaviour of the local children... [who] touched cold iron as soon as they saw any of the ministers assembled... implying that they were unlucky and dangerous people to meet" (p.104).

The Catholic Church seemed to adopt a more sympathetic attitude toward the fishermen's old-time beliefs than did the Protestants. Anson (1932) showed that in France a fishing boat which had "not been blessed by a priest is bound to be unlucky — and even anti-clerical owners are sometimes obliged to have their boats blessed lest they may find a difficulty in procuring a crew" (p.56). Whereas "in Protestant lands it is rare to find any Christian ceremony being performed in connexion with the launch of a boat, the function being limited to the semi-pagan breaking of a bottle of whiskey over the ship's side" (in Scotland — p. 57). The Pagan ritual hinted at here was the necessity of a blood sacrifice to bless the boat. Nowadays this ancient tradition is performed with champagne at the launch of a ship. The Reader's Digest (1977) concluded that even if a fisherman belonged a church ashore, many "still fear the ancient pagan gods while they are at sea. For this reason, clergymen and the Church are often forbidden topics" (p.73).

Hull's fishing community is a wonderful illustration of this dilemma. A retired trawler mate mentioned that the reason why clergymen were feared was because they dressed in black (a colour associated with death). Another trawlerman (at Hull's Trinity House Rest Homes) pointed out that it was the minister's dog-collar which caused the upset. In praiseworthy terms he claimed that the last Pastor of the Fishermen's Bethel respected the men's superstition in that he, Tom Chappell, "always wore his collar and tie whenever he visited the dock" (see photograph). At the time, I was very impressed by this story and

48

*This is a historic picture of Bethel Pastor Tom Chappell actually on St. Andrew's Dock. A universal fishing taboo is that it is unlucky for a trawlerman to meet a minister before setting sail. Tom and his wife Elsie were both Salvation Army officers at Madeley Street prior to taking up their post at the Bethel in 1938 (until 1969 when Tom died). The respected pastor was close to the Hull fishing families. His main duty being to 'break the news' to the next-of-kin of men lost at sea.*
Courtesy Elsie Chappell.

quickly scribbled it down. But on reflection, it occurred that perhaps the pastor never wore a dog-collar at anytime. The Bethel was non-denominational. This situation was subsequently confirmed by Tom's son Jeff. Nevertheless, the fact that it was falsely believed that Tom was politely bowing to superstition indicates the depth of this view amongst some Hessle Roaders.

This anti-church taboo provides a telling clue into the source of many superstitions. It highlights the guilt faced by fishermen in countries where Christianity finds it difficult to accept ancient patterns of belief. Ashore, most Hull trawlermen and their families mainly became involved with religious ministers for baptisms, weddings, and funerals (Hatched, Matched and Dispatched). But afloat, the crewmen paid an unspoken debt to the paganistic sea gods of the deep.

The spiritually-torn fishermen, therefore, evolved a secret linguistic code and taboo words are an example of this quandary. Their pagan-laden words (pig, rabbit) were disguised as alternatives (grunter, jacko). Equally, they suppressed Christian-related words (church, chapel). This word magic and disguised duality also manifested itself in the trawlermen's colourful nicknames.

# Chapter 10

## NICKNAME GAME

QUOTE: *A nickname is the heaviest stone that the*
*Devil can throw at a man.* (William Hazlitt)

In the fishing world it was not just animals, objects, and religious words which were taboo and generated alternatives. Most trawlermen had a substitute name to that of their own — a nickname. Few, if any, realised that this trawling tradition sprang from superstition. Here are a few such nicknames without any detailed explanation of their dynamic origins: Alamein Eddie, Bring-'em-Back-Alive Bob, Cod-Eyes White, Iceland Bert, The Lash, Norwegian George, Old Fox, Russian Alec, Snowy Worthington, Stalberg Ghost, Suicide Sid, Truthful George, and the White Negro.

Len Enevoldson, a former office worker with Lord Line, says that, "The top skippers were folk heroes on Hessle Road. And the popular ones were known by their first name — like Silent George". Hull skippers who trawled Iceland's North West grounds off the Nord Cap were collectively known as The Black Knights; while those who favoured the S.E. coast were The White Knights. When a skipper quietly sneaked away from the fishing ground without telling anyone which market he was steaming for, recalls Jim Fuller, he was a Carpet Slipper Merchant. An affectionate term for a skipper was The Old Man. While the boss of a trawler firm was The Gaffer.

Elsewhere in the trawler hierarchy the term for a wireless operator is Sparks. The cook is a Pan Artist. Deckhands were, on Grimsby trawlers at least, The Brats (Hutchinson, 1938, p.147). A Grimmie is a trawler or crewman from Grimsby. Lowestoft fisherman are Pudds, and Swannies come from Swansea. Germans are Square Heads. And Yorkie (for Yorkshire) is the name for a Hull crewman or trawler.

Certain Hessle Road families also have nicknames which span the generations. For example, any member of the Andrews family at sea are known as 'Shimmy'. Chief engineer Chris Hardy and his sea-going brothers are still, for some unknown reason, called 'Skadge' by their mates. More than three generations of Ron Haines' family bear the title of 'Sweat' Haines. No one knows from where or how this uncomplimentary name originated.

The nicknaming habit is so deep that it does not stop at family names. The names of some fishing grounds are not those which correspond with the navigation charts. Examples are Mother Bailey's bank, The Iron Foundry, Cow & Calf, and Bumping Ground. What must be remembered, of course, is that the pioneering skippers who opened up these distant-water grounds often did so without any detailed charts — names then passed from one generation of skippers to the next. The stretch of the northern Atlantic between Scotland and Iceland is The Pond — a euphemism, because these can be savage waters in

There was an expression in Hull which went: "You can always tell a trawlerman in town". This comment refers to the fact that most crewmen dressed very smartly in their 'fishermen's uniform'. Here is Chris Hardy (left) looking very classy (c.1930s). At sea he was chief engineer Skadge. This family nickname was given to him and all his sea-going brothers. He is on the right of the picture (below) playing his trumpet aboard the **St. Amant** (H.42 – c.1962). Skipper Alf 'Cut-throat' Smith blew down to him, "Get the band out Skadge, we've got a big halibut" – the white fish hung up behind the accordionist. Courtesy Chris Hardy.

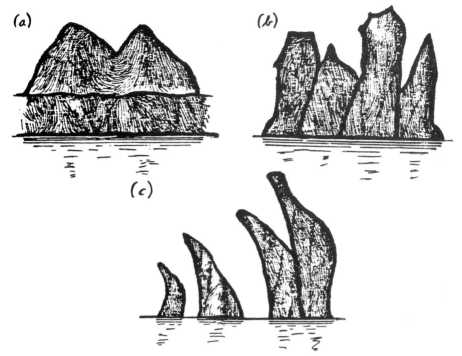

*(a) TWO HAYSTACKS (or Heimaey) can be seen on the main Westmann Island (Vestmannaeyjar –south of Iceland). There are about 20 small islands – nicknames for some of the others are The Lion, Hen & Chicken, and Jumbo.*
*(b) CHURCH ROCK is the trawlermen's nickname for Londrangar in Faxe Bay, Iceland – viewed from the north-east. This is a surprising alternative word because 'church' is a tabooed utterance (Ch. 9).*
*(c) FOUR FINGERS are at the Iron Foundry fishing ground on the south coast – the Icelandic name is Thridrangar (seen here from the north-east). This tricky ground is best trawled during the day or by the light of a full moon.*
Courtesy Albert Close.

the winter months. The White Sea grounds, geographically speaking, are really the Barents Sea, off northern Russia.

Equally, the jutting rocks by which a skipper navigated his ship to trawl a particular ground also had colourful names: Tree Stump, Lion, Two Fingers, Hen & Chicken, and Flour Sack. These names came mainly from the physical appearance as seen from the wheelhouse. Certain features of the Icelandic land-mass were named Soldier's Camp, Two Haystacks, The Beehives, and Teddies.

The different species of fish caught by the men also had camouflage names. John Crimlis reeled off fifteen fish alternatives. Some of these are: Dux for haddock, Green for cod, Black for coley, Tommies for catfish, Whips for blue ling, Soldiers for bergylt, and Table-toppers for a huge plaice.

Trawler names too were made shorter or given playful alternatives. Instead of *Arctic Avenger* (H.118) some people just say *Avenger*. Similarly with all the Kingston boats, like *Kingston Jade* (H.149), her last name only is used. Often, the recurring thematic fleet name is dropped. Some trawlers have rhyming slang names like the *Cape Matapan* (H.238) it is still referred to by some as the *Cape Watacan* — she leaked so much. Mate Bill Ward considered her a 'bad sea ship'. Incidentally, her H. registration number adds up to number thirteen — perhaps an extra worry for some trawlermen. John Crimlis calls the *Langland Bay* (H.209) the *Langland Plank* — another poor sea ship which floated heavily in the water like a saturated plank — waves easily washed over her.

To sum up this strange work-a-day world, we have a set of Hull trawlermen (Yorkies) who rarely used each others proper names, seldom refer to the correct geographical places for either the fishing grounds or landmarks, have joke names for the fish they catch, and only occasionally state the full or correct name of their trawler. Obviously, most professions and trades have their own jargon. This lingo is a useful short-hand between those in the know and can exclude outsiders. But within the wondrous world of trawling, it has been taken to extraordinary lengths. Deception leads to outright lying — another trait in the trawling trade.

# Chapter 11

## 'NEVER DIVULGE'

GAMBLING EXPRESSION: *Keep your cards close to your chest.*

The airwaves at the distant-water grounds were full of downright lies about what each skipper had or had not caught. I was told recently, "Trawlermen never divulge!". They never fully let on what they knew. It was so much part of the job that it became second nature. I wish to argue that this deception was motivated more by superstition than was generally realised. In essence, it was 'lying for luck'.

There are plenty of *practical* reasons why the truth was not told. If a skipper broadcasted that he was 'on the fish', then very soon his private patch of the sea would be swarming with trawlers — 'like Waterloo Station'. He would be deprived of landing a good catch at Hull — and thus diminish the prospects of himself and his crew getting good 'settlings'. It was in everyone's interest that the skipper lied about what was in his fish room. The logical argument, therefore, is that it is common sense to lie — it has nothing to do with superstition.

Research, however, indicates otherwise. There is a deeper, universal motive for this false information being bandied about at all levels. If the above logical argument is correct, then there is no reasonable need for deception *within* the trawler itself. That is, between the skipper and the man he worked closest with — his mate. Even they failed to communicate what was on board their own trawler. Now that is illogical. It can only stem from superstitious beliefs.

A telling case is provided by Hugh Popham (1957) in his book *CAPE OF STORMS: Trawling off the Coast of North Russia.* He was a friend of the skipper Laurie Oliver and sailed with him aboard the *Brucella* (H.291) to the White Sea in October 1955. Popham noted that when the skipper sized up the latest haul he spoke in terms of baskets — "A bare eighty baskets" — a quantity he entered into his personal log. Whereas the mate, who stowed the catch in the fish room, spoke of kits (ten stone in weight). Both men kept their own calculations as the voyage progressed. But "At any stage, the whole subject is surrounded by taboos and governed by the strictest etiquette". It was the mate's responsibility to know exactly how much fish was aboard. He was the one who provided the figures radioed to the owners as they steamed back to the Hull market. "But he would not dream of telling the skipper unless he were asked; and then his answer is likely to be vague and cautiously conservative. The skipper knows... But he will observe an almost superstitious silence on the subject" (pp.79-80).

The superstitious motive for this not-divulging taboo is 'as old as the oceans'. The unconscious fear of speaking about the amount of fish caught (killed) was to avoid the sea gods from realising what the men had extracted from the waters. The whole superstitious charade was to fool the sea gods. Furthermore, the fish themselves are living creatures with souls, and the belief was that they would wreak havoc upon their killers unless a whole pantomime of pretence was performed. The men were unwittingly protecting their own souls from having to make a sacrifice to the sea gods for the 'living' they made out of the sea, and from the revengeful off-spring of the fish they slaughtered (Ch. 29).

## Chapter 12

## WORDS HAVE POWER

BIBLE: *In the beginning was the Word.* (John 1:1)

The previous four chapters have focused upon the superstitious aspects of letters, names and words. An attempt is now made to trace the origins of these diverse beliefs. A crucial motive for avoiding taboo and proper names is based upon the pre-historic belief that 'words have power'. Anthropological research provides many examples from around the world to support the view that nicknames were used to mislead vengeful spirits. In our examination of the origins of this 'fog of deception', we will look at three areas: personal-name taboo; 'lying for luck'; and a curious Scandinavian folk tale.

Frazer (1922) showed that a native North American (Indian) "regards his name not as a mere label, but as a distinct part of his personality ... and believes that injury will result from malicious handling of his name as from a wound inflicted on any part of his physical organism" (p.244). Another tribe believe that "if you write a man's name down you can carry off his soul along with it". Australian aborigines never mention a person's true name "except upon the most solemn occasions". Even then elaborate precautions are taken and the name only whispered within a close group (p.245). Similarly with ancient Egyptian and Brahman children who were given two names: a great and a little one. Only the latter was made public. Therefore, by having a general nickname, the Hull trawlermen were unconsciously protecting their real name from any revengeful sea/fish spirits who may do them harm should their true identity become known.

In addition to nicknames for men and ships (described earlier), there was a 'smoke screen' of misleading names for the fishing grounds, landmarks, and places. Furthermore, lies were told between skippers who 'never divulged', while at sea, what they had caught; and even the skipper and mate were reluctant to state what they had in their own fish room; and deckhands rarely used the proper names of the fish they gutted. This high level of false information can be seen in superstitious terms of 'lying for luck'. Lies were told as a form of self-protection, and to increase their luck in catching more fish (Ch. 30).

A third path in the search for the origin of this deceptive process takes us to a colourful Scandinavian folk story. Once upon a time there was a giant Norse troll whose secret name was Wind & Weather. He agreed to build King Olaf a wonderful church in exchange for the Sun and the Moon. It was well known that "Anyone who managed to learn a troll's name had the power to destroy him by repeating it" (Blackcat, 1988, p.56). The building went ahead and as it neared completion the goodly king was worried about how to pay the troll's impossible wage. Then, by a stroke of luck which can only occur in sagas, Olaf

57

discovered the troll's true name. On the day the church was complete, the King yelled out, "Hold, O Wind & Weather, you've set the spire askew!". With that, the giant troll thundered to the ground, reduced to a large heap of flints. Mythical Norwegian legends such as these would filter through into the universal unconscious of European fishermen, and fortify the idea of using protective nicknames.

Some Hull trawlermen were proud of their nickname, even if it was derogatory. Chapter Three of *Good Old Hessle Road* is about the World War One naval hero 'Mad' Rilatt. His proper and grand name was Edward Spencer Rilatt the Second. It is doubtful if anyone outside his immediate family (and officialdom) knew the skipper's true name. Ted's uncomplimentary nickname came from his violent temper which could whip up without warning. In a frantic rage, he flung his cap to the deck and jumped up and down on it as he shouted abuse at some poor deckhand. The fact that he took a pride in his bravo name is shown by his reply whenever asked, "What do they call you, then, mate?". To which he gave his usual response, "Rilatt's the name. And, if you must know, it's 'Mad' Rilatt!" (Gill, 1991, p.27).

Even ashore in the fishing community places have nicknames. One which is taken for granted is the fishermen's pub on Hessle Road. Since opening in 1882, its official name was *Star & Garter*. Initially it was nicknamed 'Cartwright's' —this being the name of the very first landlord George from 1882-1910 (Gill & Sargeant, 1985, p.27). Henry Rayner was the landlord there from 1921 to 1939, and since then it has been known as 'Rayner's'. This nickname was so powerful and well-entrenched that Mansfield Brewery renamed the pub *Rayners* after a fire gutted part of the building and the place was refurbished in 1988. Other Hessle Road pubs also have local names like 'Miller's' for *Dairycoates Inn*, and the *Criterion* is shortened to 'Cri'.

Even Board Schools had sub-cultural titles such as the West Dock Avenue School which was known to some as Fish Dock College. It was close to St. Andrew's Dock and some of the older lads worked as barrow boys during their summer holidays. If dad was a trawlerman, there was a good chance he would take his son on a 'pleasure trip' to get the sea salt into his blood. The nearby Scarborough Street School decided to go one better with its nickname: Fish Dock University. Streets too had local alternatives: Gillett Street was 'Razor-Blade Alley', and The Boulevard was 'Skipper's Alley'.

All in all, the seaboard habit of dubbing people, ships and places with substitutes did not stop at the lockgates, but spilled over into the fishing community itself. The net result being that it cloaked the fishing fraternity's language and activities in a veil of mystery.

# Chapter 13

## SECRET SUPERSTITIONS

RIDDLE: *What has a thousand thousand knots*
*And a thousand thousand holes?*
*– A trawl net.* (Yugoslavian)

### *TATTOO TABOO*

Tattoos have long been associated with mariners, and most Hull trawlermen had them too. Yet few knew that they, like nicknames, had a superstitious side.

The main comment was that "a trawlerman got tattooed so his body could be identified if washed ashore". This certainly happened with the two Williams brothers washed ashore in the Soviet Union (Ch.8). Added to this, tattoos are part of the tough male culture — especially for a young deckie-learner. A gang of trawlerlads usually went to a tattooist after a few pints. 'Skadge' Hardy mentioned that when he began as a coal trimmer (c.1925), he and his mates got tattooed at the *Earl Cardigan* — a beer-house in Fish Street off Hull's market place. An old chap called Tommy Riley did tattooing in exchange for a few pints. Tommy's tattoo machine, in a box, was battery-powered with a vibrating needle. Some of Skadge's — now fading tattoos — are one for his 'MOTHER', another to his wife 'LAURA'; but the most telling of all is one related directly to his dangerous occupation: 'The Sailor's Grave'. This shows a life-belt encircling a sinking ship.

Evidence linking tattoos with superstition comes from Philippa Waring (1978) who described how they were used as lucky symbols in the U. S. Navy. Yankie sailors "claim that a pig and cockerel tattooed on the left instep protects a man against drowning" (p.197) — pigs were central to the animal taboos in Hull (Ch.18). Haining (1979) also confirmed that "sailors decorating themselves with tattoos is rooted in superstition, and the belief from primitive times that such markings protect the wearer from evil spirits and misfortune". New evidence to support this old view comes from the Iceman found recently in the Alps (Sep. 1991). What surprised many was that the 5000-year old well-preserved corpse had tattoo markings on his body. One theory is that "the Iceman was a shaman who, with tattoos, amulet, and magical axe, had climbed the mountain to do ritualistic battle with evil" (Roberts, 1993, p.54).

### *LUCKY STARBOARD*

Trawlermen did various routines at sea *without* being aware that some were steeped in magic going back to the hidden depths of time.

Most Hull skippers 'chose' to shoot their trawl gear from the starboard (right) side. At the rational level Bob Rowntree neatly explains that "The starboard was best with a single-right-handed screw [propeller] ship because

59

when trawling off you get away from the gear quicker — the ship's [natural] clockwise turning circle is shorter than if the gear is over the port side". In other words, the skipper easily steamed away from the slack trawl nets without getting them tangled in the propeller blades. I am sure that this common-sense nautical view is correct. But it is not the full picture. There are two opposing reasons why fishermen the world over prefer the starboard to the port side — regardless of how the ship is powered.

A couple of New Testament accounts provide a clue to this tradition. St. John the Apostle described the sacred period after the Crucifixion when Jesus, risen from the dead, returned to see the disciples. The fishermen were unhappy because during the previous day in the Sea of Tiberius, not one single fish had been caught. Christ told them "Cast the net on the right side of the ship and ye shall find. They cast therefore and now they were not able to draw it for the multitude of fishes" (John 21:1-11). This parable has been told and re-told in Christian fishing ports — the implication being very clear if a crew want a good trip. A second biblical story is Matthew's description of The Last Judgement. Our souls will be divided as sheep on the right and goats to the left: "Then shall He say unto them on the left hand 'Depart from me, ye cursed, into everlasting fire, prepared for the devil and his angels" (Matthew 25:41).

The ancient Pagans, however, provided a simpler reason. Anything to do with the left is bad. Folklore takes its signs from Nature. The sun rises in the east. If, at the glorious crack of dawn, we face the sun and remain orientated in that direction, its warmth and goodness shine upon our right-hand side. Meanwhile, the side kept in shadow is the left. Latin for left is *sinister*. This word also describes an individual as being evil or treacherous. And Roman auguries considered the left as the unlucky side of anything (Collins).

Opie & Tatem (1989) provided examples to show that this anti-left feeling is not just found in Hull. In 1887 it was reported that fishermen on the Western Isles of Ireland "when going to sea must always enter the boat by the right side, no matter how inconvenient" (p.34). And in 1932 an angler near Perth advised "don't hold the rod in your left hand, sir! If you do there'll be no luck today!" (p.231).

The right is associated with good fortune, while the left is ill-omened. And so this left-right divide has been transferred to the earliest fishing boats and continued on to the 20th century steam, oil, and diesel side-winder trawlers from Hull. This ancient hauling taboo finally disappeared with the introduction of the modern freezers which tow their gear from the stern of the ship.


*WEATHER LORE*

"Worse things happen at sea" is a common expression in Hull. If ever I feel the weather is bad ashore, I often take comfort from this phrase. As the trawlermen's livelihood and lives depended upon the elements, they often looked out for portends in the weather. Superstition obviously mingled in with this sign searching.

Expressions like 'howling winds', 'angry waves' and 'violent storms' suggest

*Many ancient superstitions have been swept aside by 'advances' in technology. The stern-loading freezer trawler removes the skipper's dilemma over whether to fish over the port or starboard side. In the days of steam sidewinders, most skippers used only the starboard gallows because it was unlucky to haul on the left side. This scene was aboard the modern* **Cordella** *(H.177) skippered by Dick 'Old Fox' Taylor in November 1980.*
Copyright Alec Gill.

the work of a hidden malevolent hand. "In almost every ancient mythology thunder, lightning, and fierce winds have been thought of as manifestations of the gods, and usually of their anger" (Radford, 1974, p.324). Out of this belief came 'weather lore' or 'weather magic'. As far as Hull trawlermen were concerned, there were some little rhymes which helped them remember the signs (probably handed down from sailing-smack days). John Crimlis tells of one:

*"When birds fly low*
*The wind will blow."*

Bill Lewis has a ditty warning of bad weather ahead:

*"When the wind backs against the sun*
*Trust it not, for back it will run."*

When the wind blows in an anti-clockwise direction, or a 'contrary wind' as described by seafarers of old, there is trouble ahead (Rappoport, 1930, p.5). In folk lore jargon the word Widdershins is used, meaning 'against the sun'. This left-ward, anti-clockwise, turn again reveals the bias against anything associated with left-handedness (as with port-side). Nevertheless, this superstitious sign has a basis of logic in the northern hemisphere in that anti-cyclone winds can develop into hurricanes which are serious trouble for those at sea.

Bill Lewis added another weather lore expression:

*"When clouds are all streaky, like mare's tails.*
*It is a sign of strong winds –*
*Even the next day."*

For the women of Hessle Road with men at sea, the winter months were a time of anxiety. A woman phoned into Radio Humberside to tell how she "listened to every weather and shipping forecast, and thought about the men out at sea" (Mar. 1990).


*YULE YARN*

There is an amusing Christmas story which illustrates how bad luck (poor catches) can be blamed upon anything out-of-the-ordinary. Bob Rowntree was a young lad (18) aboard the *Lord Hewart* (H.475) in December 1938 fishing off the west coast of Iceland. The deckhands were bored with hardly any fish to gut. So, for a bit of fun, they built a Father Christmas in the fo'c'sle — dressed in red, with a hat, beard and all his regalia. He was erected on the escape ladder which gave the effect of a Christmas tree. A few days later skipper Bert Hume happened to see the Santa Claus. "He went barmy, and ordered the hands to get rid of him". Bert declared, "It's because of that White Whiskered Old Bastard that we're not catching any fish".

# Chapter 14

## CORPSE ON BOARD

PROVERB: *Our last garment is made without pockets.*

There is usually an implied threat that if a superstition is not followed, the transgressor will be punished. The most serious punishment is DEATH. In this sense, death is the bedrock of many superstitions.

When sickness and death were close at hand, those of a superstitious nature were on the look out for ominous signs. If a crewman fell seriously ill or injured it was believed that he would not pass away until land was sighted. A suicide on board cast a black shadow over the trawler. Radio 'sparks' Ron Haines said "it created a strange aura over the crew. And some men joined a different trawler on their next trip". Ron added that if a deckhand was lost overboard, this could demoralise the men. Some skippers got the gear on board and steamed home so that everyone could start afresh. "No good can come out of it if someone is washed over — very superstitious" he concluded.

If ever a corpse was hauled up and fell out of the cod-end, not unusual in post-war years, it also had a disturbing effect. If a drowned fishermen laid on his belly, he was quickly turned over — it was unlucky for him to be face down. If the trawled-up body was long-decayed, the corpse was quickly tossed back into the sea to avoid getting involved with red tape ashore. Fishermen in general feel it unlucky to have a corpse on board — as we saw with the Williams brothers and the crewmen who refused to collect their bodies from Russia (Ch. 8). When a body is buried at sea, "they will not look as it disappears beneath the waves. If they do, superstition says they will soon follow it" (Waring, 1978, p. 66).

Ron Haines was aboard the *Rossella* (H.336) when the *Norman* (H.289) was wrecked at Greenland's Cape Farewell on 4 October 1952. Eight of the *Norman's* crew managed to struggle onto a reef, but only one lad survived. The mutilated bird-pecked bodies of the rest were picked up by the *Thornella* (H.582 — Skipper Charlie O'Neill). As the *Rossella* passed her sister ship, the skipper ordered the trawler's flag be lowered to half-mast as a sign of respect.

As the *Thornella* steamed toward Britain, no one was keen to go anywhere near the corpses on the boat deck. The seven bodies had been packed in ice in the two tarpaulin-covered lifeboats. At 4.00 a.m. one morning sparehand Ken Johnson and deckhand George Woods were arguing on the bridge. Neither man wanted to go in the dark to read the ship's log which was towed from the trawler's boat deck. Both men were frightened to do this routine job. It was, however, George who ended up leaving the wheelhouse, clutching a torch to get the reading. By sheer coincidence, it so happened that cook Horace Brookes, dressed as usual in his white clothes and apron, came up through the accommodation hatch onto the boat deck. Even he was on tenterhooks, but he

63

*The crushed wheelhouse of the **Thornella** (H.582) was caused by a hurricane on 9 January 1953. On the bridge is bosun Herbert Howlett (left) and skipper Charlie O'Neill. A few trips prior, Charlie had brought back seven bodies from the **Norman** (H.289) lost in October 1952 at Greenland. Although the skipper was not superstitious, an older relative became worried that the **Thornella** was an ill-fated ship after carrying the corpses. In an eerie sort of way, this storm damage can be seen as a fulfilment of this foreboding.*
Courtesy Raymond Johnson.

had to get some beef from the salt cask. When they both came face to face they almost frightened each other to death. The story goes that poor George was still shaking a week later. Charlie O'Neill recalls that, "the log never got read that morning". The skipper was wary about bringing the bodies all the way back to Hull; so they were landed at Scrabster (Caithness) in Scotland.

Although O'Neill is not the superstitious sort, an older relative was worried that Charlie would be unlucky on that ship because corpses had been on board. On January 9th the next year the *Thornella* was struck by a hurricane and her wheel-house crushed in (see photograph). One final superstition was that if ever a body was brought ashore, the corpse must leave before any member of the crew.

# PART THREE
## ANIMALS


### Chapter 15
### MAGIC CREATURES

HYMN: *All things bright and beautiful,*
*All creatures great and small.*
(Cecil Alexander)

In fishing folklore animals have magical properties and give mystical messages. Birds are the souls of the dead. Cats foretell storms. Pigs are venerated. Rabbits symbolise fertility. Rats desert a sinking ship. Dogs sense death. And each species of fish has its own mythology.

Humans have a deep bond with the animal kingdom. Most Zodiac signs are animal. Each Chinese New Year centres around a different species. National stereotypes (or totems) depict a fearsome beast: the Russian bear, American eagle, British bulldog (or lion), and the Chinese dragon. Some people think of themselves as being re-incarnated as an animal (I have an affinity with the cormorant). Not surprisingly, animals loom large in the superstitious thinking of the earliest fishermen. So entrenched is this imagery, that it continues to strike a chord in the minds of the modern Hull trawlermen.

The strongest evidence of animal superstitions is found in taboo words which must never be uttered aboard a trawler. But that aspect is just the tip of the proverbial iceberg. Delving into the academic literature there is wider support for this Hull phenomena. Anson (1932) claimed, "On the Yorkshire coast all four-footed animals are regarded with equal disfavour" (p.86). Rappoport (1930) highlighted hares, rats, pigs, cats "and sometimes also dogs, horses and spiders" (p.25). The last two have not been found during my interviews. But, for the Hull families, this list is only complete if we add birds and fish. Regardless of species, it is an unlucky omen to see any drowned animal. The sheer size of the animal section in this book reflects the influence magic creatures had in Hull's superstitious heritage.

*I do not know why, but seagulls are nicknamed 'mollies'. Three gulls seen flying together*
*are an ominous sign of death. Rhea (1985) mentioned that gulls*
*"contain the souls of the drowned and that their cries are cries of the dead warning*
*the living against storms and hidden dangers" (p.24-25). This 'molly' is perched*
*on the fore-mast derrick of a Hull trawler.*
Courtesy Gary Bennett.

# Chapter 16

## 'WINGED MESSENGERS'

RHYME: *If the gulls are out,*
*Then luck is about.* (French)

At sea or ashore there is an ominous aura around birds. In the Hessle Road homes there was a strong bird taboo amongst the women. A common remark, even today, is "I'll never have any birds in my house". This attitude is sometimes contradictory. Cordelia Jones was brought up by a grandmother who said one thing, but did another. She firmly stated, "No birds are allowed in this house". Yet they had a canary. Her aversion was toward bird ornaments, pictures, wallpaper, or furnishings. School-leaver John Crimlis, just starting to bring a wage packet home, happily bought a present for his step-mother. Naïvely it was three flying swans to hang on the wall. She quickly grabbed the pot ornaments from him and angrily threw the birds into the back-yard dustbin saying that it was unlucky to bring things like that into the house — without giving a reason why. One lady told about her aunt in Hawthorn Avenue who actually "had wallpaper with birds on — it was so rare". No doubt other members of her family expected dire things to happen to this aunt at any time.

Doreen Fleet says that whenever she buys a box of assorted Christmas cards, "any with a bird on get thrown out" — the poor robins end up in the bin. This bird taboo has financial consequences for the Hessle Road traders. Marsh Nicholson furniture-shop owner George Nicholson commented, "We never stocked anything like pots, eiderdowns or pictures with birds on". Phyllis Price in the nearby Henry Hird Jewellers told how, "People are very susperstitious. They never buy China with a bird design on — it is like part of their soul".

This telling remark gives the vital clue: birds are harbingers of death — especially for families with men at sea. This view is summed up by Stan Futty of Gipsyville, "If a bird comes in the house, especially one falling down the chimney, it means ill-tidings. Mother wouldn't have anything with a bird on it". In the days of open coal fires it was not unknown for a bird to accidentally drop down the chimney. This startling event would, in itself, cause quite a fright. But with the death-laden warning attached it, a high degree of foreboding could follow in a superstitious household. Even Shakespeare described the portentous bird as a 'hooting and shrieking' harbinger (Julius Caeser, Act I/iii/26).

Another feared omen is if a bird taps at the window or flaps wildly against it in a panic. This is a clear message from the soul of a drowned trawlerman — letting someone in his family know that he had just departed this life. This after-death bird-tap has also been reported abroad. "All around the coast of Brittany it is held almost universally that if a man dies at sea his wife will be warned of the fact in some supernatural manner — e.g., by a bird knocking at

# WHITESIDE

## (Prop. : A. G. DEWEY)

## 297ᴬ, HESSLE ROAD.

### Corner of Harrow Street.

## LIVESTOCK, GOLDFISH, CORN, AND BIRD SEEDS. : : CANARIES AND GENUINE AFRICAN GREY PARROTS.

**Always on hand—LARGE STOCK OF CAGES, Etc.**

*Superstition and contradiction go together. When it came to having a bird in a Hessle Road home, there was certainly a double standard at work. Bird ornaments, pictures, and wall-paper were definitely forbidden. But a bird was alright as a domestic pet. So the Whiteside Pet Shop may have done a brisk trade with their African Grey Parrots. The Dewey family ran this business for fifty years from 1932.*
Courtesy Chris Ketchell.

the window...Very often she will refuse to believe in the death of her son or husband unless she has received an *avinement* or warning" (Anson, 1932, pp. 41-42).

Besides being in awe of the bird's remarkable gift of flight, earth-bound mortals also see the bird as a heavenly messenger. Radford (1974) pointed out that, "Priests and soothsayers of pagan antiquity [including the Romans] studied birds' flight, cries and actions in order to read the future and discover whether any proposed enterprise would turn out well or ill" (p.50). The practice of ornithomancy — divination by birds — has long been repressed by the established church. Yet a sublimated form of bird divination is alive not only in folklore superstition, but also in nursery rhymes. The belief that the future can be foretold by the behaviour of birds is evident in the Magpie verse sung by children:

*"One for sorrow*
*Two for joy*
*Three for a girl*
*Four for a boy... "*

In some parts of the country, people spit or salute if they see a single magpie to avert bad luck. When we use the expression 'a little birdie told me...' it has its roots in this type of belief. Finally, from the land-lubbers point of view, there is a Yorkshire rhyme which sees the bird as a forecaster of weather to come. When the gulls are seen inland, the saying goes:

*"Seagull, seagull get on to sand*
*It'll never be fine while you're on land"*

Looking back on his long seafaring career, chief engineer 'Skadge' Hardy describes the gull as "The trawlermen's only company at sea". Some trawlermen say it is uncanny the way the gulls, gannets, and petrels suddenly appear from nowhere whenever they began to haul in their trawl gear. But 'Skadge' explains away the bird's 'intuitive knowledge' by pointing out that they simply heard the sound of the winch machinery starting up and arrive 'out of the blue' to get their pickings.

The ominous seagull figured in the minds of many trawlermen. One such was bosun George Allan, who sailed mainly aboard the *Lord Mountevans* (H.169). He stated that the "seagulls should never be killed because they are the souls of dead fishermen in torment". One nickname for gulls is 'mollies'.

The belief that it is unlucky to kill a seabird is echoed in the Coleridge (1798) poem *The Rime of the Ancient Mariner* whereby the old man "had done a hellish thing" by killing the albatross. With a hint of irony in his voice, Charles Ayre — owner of the Humber motor launch *Kitty* who ferried the crewmen about — remarked, "They never reckoned to shoot seagulls at seas". He never did elaborate, but the implication was that it did happen sometimes. A few years later, I heard the yarn of a nasty skipper who frequently shot 'mollies'. He often took an air-rifle to sea. When fishing was slack, the bored skipper loaded up with pellets and took a perverse pleasure in firing from the wheel-house at any gull resting on the ship's rigging. Needless to say, he was unpopular with many of the crew.

Skipper Harry Taylor described a trick played on the seabirds by some deckhands. With hundreds of gannets dive-bombing onto the waves to grab any bits of offal it was easy to fool the poor creatures. Two fish were securely tied together with a piece of twine and hurled overboard. Before the fish had chance to hit the water each was savagely gulped by a seabird. The cruel joke was that the two birds were then fixed together as they flapped about in mid-air. Neither could escape until one regurgitated its portion.

Most deckhands, however, were sympathetic toward their Arctic companions. Ted Rilatt (junior) recalls that racing pigeons from the Continent sometimes landed exhausted on a trawler. They usually died because they had swallowed too much salt water. Sometimes mollies dropped on to the deck, unable to get airborne again. Sheltered in the fish pounds, there was not enough breeze to lift them off the ship again. In these circumstances, deckhands tried to get hold of the helpless birds to throw them up in to a gust of air. But they had to be careful not to get a vicious bite from the sharp beaks.

Bosun Brian Williams hated birds. The story of his tragic death brings together many of the Hessle Road bird taboos. We saw earlier how he lost two of his older brothers aboard the *Boston Lincoln* (GY.1399) when Harry Williams jumped into the White Sea to save Terry and both were lost. After a long saga the Soviets returned the bodies of these two brothers and they were buried alongside each other in Hull's Northern Cemetery (Ch. 8). Whenever Brian visited their graves, he got angry if he saw bird droppings on their head-stones. When talking about his brothers, he once told his wife Evelyn, "It'll happen to me yu'know" — he truly believed he would die at sea.

On the rainy afternoon of 25 May 1976, Evelyn decided to visit her mother-in-law Hilda at No. 45 Edinburgh Street. Brian and Evelyn were childhood sweet-hearts and played together in Hilda's house as kids. Ironically, this was a significant day for the Williams family. After two long years, the outstanding legal claims for compensation were finally settled for the widows of Terry and Harry Williams. That wet afternoon (2.30 p.m.) the women's chatter was abruptly stopped by a rustling noise from behind the gas-fire. Hilda declared, "Oh! I hate that!". Two birds had fallen down the stack. The women dared not get the trapped birds out from behind the boarded-up fireplace. They were left until the men came home. Evelyn is not superstitious so did not give it too much heed.

Unbeknown to them, that was the exact time when Brian was killed aboard the *St. Benedict* (H.164). Again, it was at the White Sea. And again there was a problem with the trawl gear. Brian hooked the jumbo gilson and signalled the mate on the winch to take the slack. But there was too much strain. The tension rove at the ring bolt which shot out and hit Brian on the back of his head with such force that he was killed outright.

At 6.30 p.m. Evelyn recognised Supt. David Saltiel and his colleague outside her house at No. 67 Rugby Street. She wondered, "Where are they going?". When Evelyn answered the door she innocently asked, "What's he done?". David simply shook his head. After all the tragedy to strike the Williams family this was a billion-to-one situation — three brothers killed at sea. Evelyn knew from his silent expression that Brian's gloomy foreboding had come true.

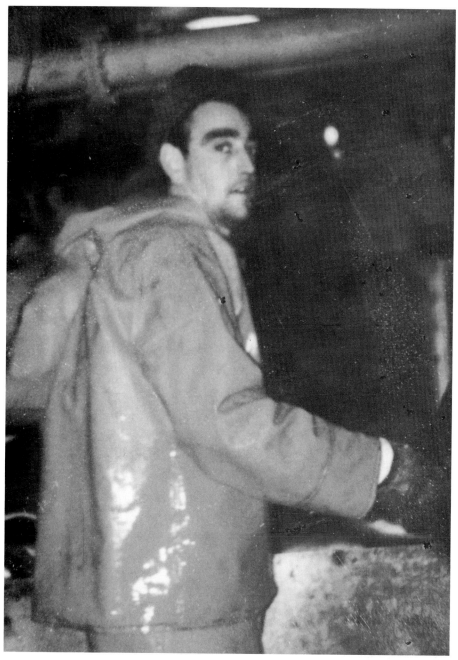

*This (slightly blurred) picture of Brian Williams shows him in the factory of the **St. Benedict** (H.164). He was killed in an accident aboard this ship (25 May 1976) just a week before his 31st birthday. Prior to setting sail his daughter Julie was due to start school. Brian was proud to take her to the gates of West Dock Avenue School on her big day. His wife Evelyn commented, "All the Williams brothers lived for their kids". After a pause she added, "I feel cheated. He was not there to see his kids grow up and share in their achievements".*
Courtesy Evelyn Williams.

*We hear about coal-miners taking canaries down the pits to warn against gas; but I have never heard of Hull trawlermen taking a bird to sea. This 1948 scene, aboard a Marr trawler, was a bit of a mystery. Later research found that the bird had been rescued by Hull trawlermen from the Dutch coaster **Weskus**, which was adrift in the North Sea with a bad list after the coal shifted in the hold. The crew had abandoned ship and left this caged canary to fend for herself.*
Courtesy Robert Ramsbottom.

Then a second ominous bird superstition occurred. After the Mission men had left, she noticed something strange had happened to one of the three pot wild geese ornaments she had on her living-room wall. The middle one had somehow smashed to pieces.

Meanwhile, back at the White Sea, the *St. Benedict* headed toward Kirkeness Island, off Norway. Brian's body was put ashore so that the freezer trawler could continue her fishing trip. Then history (and superstition) cruelly repeated itself for the devastated Williams family. No Hull trawler would collect the corpse to bring Brian home for burial. It was a fortnight before either a cargo or naval vessel brought him back to England.

Evelyn recalls that despite Brian's bird phobia, there was one species he liked. They were mollies. If any landed distressed on his trawler he would help them back into the air to see them on their way — maybe he felt they carried the souls of his drowned brothers.

Any black-coloured bird is viewed with suspicious eyes, especially the raven. In the pre-WWI days, when the North Sea boxing fleets were Hull's main source of fish, it was believed that if a raven croaked as the boats left St. Andrew's Dock, then the voyage would be unlucky. A related view is that it is bad luck if a raven is seen to the left, especially early in the morning. Hull's enormous Gamecock Fleet, owned by Kelsall Brothers & Beeching, seemed oblivious of this maritime taboo. They named most of their trawlers after birds like *Eagle* (H.454) and *Swallow* (H.97). They even had one called *Raven* (H.858) — but I have not heard of it being unlucky!

It is not only trawlermen who are superstitious. The United Kingdom has a national taboo about the raven. It is believed that if ever the ravens leave the Tower of London, then Britain will be invaded and doomed. So as not to take any chances, the Beefeaters clip the wings of the portentous royal black birds.

The seafaring and folklore associations with birds goes on and on. Many of the beliefs about birds can be traced back to Celtic-Roman times when ornithomancy was at its height. The Celts saw birds as the "companions of the gods" (Blackcat, 1988, p.138). Anne Ross (1974) wrote about raven lore — a bird of great importance to the Celts as a means of divination: "future events were frequently divined from the flight and cries of ravens...otherworld ravens were the invariable bearers of evil tidings" (p.327). Similarly, Hull's 20th century trawlermen and their families looked for good and bad signs in the flight of birds.

# Chapter 17

## NINE LUCKY LIVES

POEM: *What Cat is averse to fish?* (Thomas Gray)

The enigmatic cat easily stalks her way into the shadow of superstition. And, in the sphere of magic, our feline friend has been treated as everything from a Deity to a Devil. Not surprisingly, therefore, she figures in the various beliefs of Hull's trawlermen. I stress the seafarers because they are the source of most of the Hull tales which have come my way. No one in the community specifically mentioned any anecdotes about cats.

For shore-based taboos I turned to material from the literature. One reference told about the wives of Yorkshire fishermen who liked to keep a black cat at home so that "her man will return safely from sea" (Radford, 1974, p. 87). And, if there was a death in the family, the cat disappeared until after the funeral (Maple, 1980, p. 421). A noteworthy point is that the British Isles is unique in its attitude toward whether a black cat is lucky or unlucky. In the U.S.A. and most European countries, the white cat is lucky, while black is synonymous with Satan. Only the British speak of 'The Lucky Black Cat'.

The golden rule for Hull's deep-sea trawlermen was never to chase a cat off the ship. Otherwise it would take its nine lucky lives with it. Some crewmen took their own domestic cat like the cook of the *Admiral Collingwood* (H.341). But it was an even better omen if a cat strayed aboard of her own accord. Despite the desire to have this creature on board, the word 'Cat' was taboo. As yet, I have not traced an alternative name — perhaps that is where 'moggie' comes in. It was unlucky, however, to have two cats aboard the same ship.

In the 1930s, an un-named skipper broke the most serious cat superstition of all. After a long run of bad trips and in a rage of pent up frustration, he strangled the ship's cat because she had not brought him any luck. The feeling on St. Andrew's Dock, echoed by motor-launch owner Herbert Ayre, was "He'll never have any luck after that."

The *Admiral Collingwood's* cat was called Tich. Since the ship's maiden voyage in October 1936, the cook Bill Worsey had taken his cat on the first four trips. This new generation of 'super trawler' was the pride of the port. Under the command of top skipper Fred Danton, she was about to set sail for a Christmas trip on 12 December that year. Just before Bill left his Brunswick Avenue home, he suddenly decided *not* to take Tich because "it might be too cold for the poor cat at Bear Island". His wife pleaded with him to take the cat "for luck". But Bill left Tich with his two young sons — never to see his family again. The *Collingwood* was last heard from on 30 December. In horrific gales she was smashed to pieces on the west coast of Norway, near Aalesund — with the loss of eighteen Hull crew. It is stories like this which confirm the view that cats have nine lives — well, it was certainly true for Tich.

Cats in Flinton Street were at serious risk of being taken to the Arctic Circle whether they wanted to go or not. Bosun John 'Chuffer' Harrison, whenever he was on his way to join a ship, "just took any moggie he happened to see sitting on a window-sill". Frantic neighbours rushed up to his wife Annie May yelling, "Your husband's taken our pissing cat again!".

In addition to the life-saving aura associated with cats, it was believed by some that they had supernatural powers to foretell the weather. During a fishing trip some members of the crew watched the behaviour of the ship's cat very closely. If she washed behind her ears three times, then rain was due. Should she dash about in a wild frenzy and claw viciously at the furniture, this signalled strong winds. And, if she sat with her back to the stove, a frost or even a storm was on its way. This Hull view is reflected in the wider sphere by Haining (1979). He confirmed the British position that "Cats are lucky creatures to have on board, especially all-black ones — and they also act as a weather omen, for when they are particularly lively, sailors say they have the wind in their tails and are giving warning that a storm is brewing" (p.151). The opposite view is put forward in Scandinavia where "Swedish sailors refuse to take a black cat on board, for it carries storm in its tail" (Rappoport, 1930, p. 83). The belief here is that the cat herself actually causes the storm. This thinking dates back to ancient times when cats were seen as having mystical powers to control the climate. But before we look at the origins of the cat taboos, there are a few more sea-cat tales to relate.

There are two stories told about one very lucky fish dock cat. She is un-named and the two yarns span a ten-year period. So whether it was actually the same cat, I am not absolutely sure. In August 1929, it was noticed that this cat removed all her new-born kittens from St. Andrew's Dock. The next day, Sunday 25th, some new dock buildings, still under construction, went up in flames. What people in the nearby streets remember vividly about the vast inferno was the wave of rats which swarmed from the dock to invade the community. This same cat then leaps to 1939. By this time the moggie had found her way aboard the Jutland Amalgamated trawler *Lady Jeanette* (H.466) — still with some of her nine lives intact. In addition, she managed to get herself a minder in the shape of chief engineer Frank Green (from Rosamund Street). He had a soft spot for cats and took a particular shine to the *Jeanette's* mascot. Then, in February 1939, after returning from a fishing trip, he realised that the cat had suddenly disappeared from the 472-ton side-winder. Frank also decided to follow suit and took a trip off — a fateful decision which saved his life. Upon the *Lady Jeanette's* return from the winter fishing grounds off Norway, the unpredictable Humber estuary was in an angry mood. High winds and an extraordinary strong spring tide battered the 164-foot vessel.

The *Jeanette* strained at her anchor as she awaited the high tide and the opening of the lockgates. But the force of the driving current snapped the anchor chain and swept the two-year old *Jeanette* helplessly up river. She struck a sandbank and sank in no time. Nine lives were lost, including that of the replacement chief engineer. Nancy Green tells how her husband Frank, like his feline friends, was also blessed with extra lives. Besides surviving the dangerous convoy work aboard trawlers in the Second World War, he decided to switch trawlers on about half-a-dozen occasions, just before they were lost. The most notable change being when he left the *Lorella* (H.455) in 1955. On her next trip, she iced-up and heeled over on the 26 January along with the ill-fated *Roderigo* (H.135). Despite his tremendous luck, Frank had a gut feeling that he would die at sea. It seemed that Fate had other plans. He died in bed at home aged 75 in 1981. Nancy added "he seemed disappointed to end his days that way".

It is curious that British seafarers hold a fondness for having a cat aboard ship. For centuries the cat was cast in such a weird light. She was associated with malevolent black witches. Cats were despised as a witches' familiar whereby the supposedly evil woman changed herself into the shape of a cat. In the bleak Dark Ages at the fearsome time of the witch-hunts, cats were burnt alive along with their owners in villages throughout Europe (Maple, 1980, p. 419). Our mariners' affection for the cat, however, seems rooted more in the pre-Christian times when felines were venerated. There were ancient cat cults in Egypt, Ireland and Scotland. Caithness in the far north beyond the Highlands, apparently takes its name from the clan of the Catti or 'cat-people'. The Greek goddess Diana of Nemi assumed the form of a cat. And Freya (or Frigg), the Scandinavian goddess of love and fertility, had her chariot drawn by a team of cats (Ch.24). Both these Pagan goddesses had mystical links with the moon, and so does the cat. Like the moon, the cat is a creature of the night. In the bright light of day, the cat's eyes are narrow; but at night, they shine wide open and gleam like the full moon. The cat is described "as a child of the moon" (Maple, 1980, p.417). And, as the moon controls the tides, there is an obvious link with mariners.

It was sacrilege to kill a cat in Pharaoh's Egypt. And, in a roundabout way, the 20th century Hull trawlermen honoured this tradition. It was usually understood that if a trawler was in distress, the cat must be saved first. This happened with the *St. Honorius* (H.66) owned by Thomas Hamling. She had just arrived off the north east coast of Iceland on 19 January 1933 when she struck an uncharted rock. The 1929 Beverley-built trawler sprang a leak. The small black-and-white cat of chief engineer Harness was brought up on deck. Skipper Furniss told, "the cat must have known that something was wrong. When put in the small boat it never made a move". They took this as a warning and decided to abandon ship. All fourteen crew lived to tell the tale. But what an eight-week venture it was before they were to see home again.

Despite a strong wind blowing off the land, they struggled ashore. They came across two small farms where they rested. Although very friendly, the isolated Icelanders were extremely fearful of catching influenza from England and so the men were quarantined on the farms for a month. Next followed an eight-hour sleigh journey in which the men nearly froze to death. Furniss even had icicles on his eyelashes — the men's faces blistered in the bitter cold. Next came a motorboat journey, but the awful petrol fumes made them feel sickly. Then by mail boat to Reykjavik. A few days later s.s. *Gadafoss* set sail into the teeth of a storm-force gale. When the *St. Honorius* crewmen arrived back in Hull they had only the clothes they stood up in — two of them had even lost their false teeth aboard the wrecked trawler. But their most precious item

76

*This is one of the best pictures I have come across to illustrate animal superstitions – two for the price of one. A close inspection shows the skipper in the middle with a black furry cat on his lap – given pride of place. The second lucky mascot is held by the young man on the floor to the right. He is holding a knitted white bunny rabbit. On the 13 January 1916 these 12 crewmen were mined aboard the H.M.T. **Rosy Morn** in the North Sea. They were rescued by the **Etna** (H.940). A copy of this print was presented to various people involved in their lucky escape from a watery grave.*

Courtesy Kevin Marshall (Warehouse Antiques).

which they brought with them through all their rigorous ordeal was their lucky ship's cat (HDM, 20 Mar. 33, p.1).

While cats were welcomed aboard with open arms, there was one creature which was the most feared of all by Hull trawlermen.

**Chapter 18**

## TOTEM ANIMAL

DICTIONARY: *'TOTEM' —*
*A North American Indian word for some*
*natural object, usually an animal,*
*taken as an emblem of a tribe.*
(Brewer)

It was extremely unlikely that a Hull trawlerman fishing off Bear Island, far within the frozen Arctic Circle, would ever come face to face with the next animal.

Yet of *ALL* creatures this was the most reviled. Few Hessle Roaders used its proper name — even today. Instead, some might spell it out letter by letter. Others silently mouth each letter. During a long discussion about this feared creature, one woman in my group had the fingers of both her hands tightly crossed. Later, she held them in the air and explained that it was to avert any evil influence which may strike as a result of this name being spoken aloud by others. On other occasions, telephone calls have been cut short because I happened to name this animal in passing.

As might be expected from previous superstitious behaviours, this animal too has alternative names which 'protect' the person from uttering its proper one. The fact that there are around one dozen options shows the degree of emotional feeling generated by this beast. If you have not yet guessed its name, you soon will as this list unfolds: Curly-tail, Porker, Grunter, Porky, That Grunting Animal, and Parger-Warger (similar to the childhood expression Piggy-Wiggy). Other British seafarers used words like Hog or Sow (Haining, 1979, p.149). This most awesome animal is 'p-i-g'. Even amongst people who spell out its name, there is a strange element of disguise. One woman quirkily spelt it 'p-one-g' ('p-1-g'). Beyond spelling is absolute SILENCE. The daughter of a Hull trawler mate (called Carr) tells that her dad often said, "I'm not scared of man nor beast, apart from grunter".

This taboo is the strangest one in the hundreds of Hull superstitions. But, just to put things into a wider perspective even the great and mighty have shown a deference toward our porky friend. Sir Winston Churchill is reputed to have said,

> *"Man looks down on dog.*
> *Cat looks down on man.*
> *But pig stares man in the eye*
> *And sees his equal."*

Before looking at sea stories about porker, there are a few tales about him ashore. A contradiction is that some Hessle Road families had a pigsty. Only a

78

few, that is, because not many households had a garden in their back-way. Along with geese, goats and chickens, swine were kept by three Beecroft Street families. Neighbours saved stale bread, potato-peelings and left-overs for swill. After the arrival of a new litter, the children of the street were invited to see the pink squealing piglets. On market day these youngsters were roped in to help herd the fully-grown porkers into a cart — horse-drawn in the olden days. They blocked off passage-ends to head the creatures toward the street. Other children lined up on the pavement to direct the frightened animals up a ramp —with trawl nets fixed either side — into the waiting cart.

After describing this frantic activity in the Hull *Target* newspaper (Feb. 90), I got a letter from Susan Smith about her parents' private joke. Apparently, her father had bow legs and his wife often poked fun at him saying, "You couldn't stop a pig in a passage with those legs". They then doubled over in peels of laughter and no one could get any sense out of them for ages afterwards. In Glasgow Street the kids 'accidentally' let the swine run free into the street. It was mayhem as everyone tried to capture the poor things destined for the slaughter-house (Crowther, 1987, p.6). As we found with the cat, there were no strong feelings toward curly-tail until we set off to sea.

The final community story leads us directly into the trawlermen going off to sea — or not, if they met a porker. Dora Wright, as a young woman, was donkey-stoning the door-step at her parent's house when she saw a trawlerman walking toward the fish dock with a bag over his shoulder. Then suddenly a stick-wielding neighbour herded out a hog he was taking to the cattle market. The deckhand stopped dead in his tracks and said, "That's it, I'm not going to sea today". He turned around and went back home. This Hessle Road account is confirmed in the literature by Anson (1932) who widens this superstition to the whole of the U.K.. He described how 'pig' is a taboo word all around the British coast, especially in Cornwall, Yorkshire and Scotland — "There is no animal more unlucky for fishermen" and few put to sea after seeing one (p.63). This returning-home aspect, however, dramatically highlights a conflict between two taboos. We saw with sailing-day superstitions that it was an ill omen to 'turn back' after setting off for the ship (Ch.7). Yet here is a situation which forced a fisherman to return home. As well as showing the contradictory nature of superstitions, this also illustrates how the power of the pig taboo over-rides other rituals. Furthermore, it indicates that there is a pecking-order within the beliefs themselves — with pigs being very high in the hierarchy.

How then did Hull trawlermen 'encounter' old curly-tail in the unlikely context of their work on the Arctic boats? I have limited myself here to only three specific trawling tales. The first relates to skipper Ernie Clark of the *Lord Bradbury* (H.251). He adamantly refused to have anything to do with pork on his ship. Bob Rowntree was part of his crew in 1937 as she steamed off in the Humber. Amongst the joints of meat being stowed below on the ice in the fish room was a pig's head. Whether it was a mean joke or merely an accident we may never know; but "Ernie went bloody barmy — no doubt about it". He immediately turned the 338-ton trawler around and headed straight back into St. Andrew's Dock. He refused to sail until 24-hours had passed. Trawler owners Pickering & Haldane "just had to accept the situation". Skipper Clark

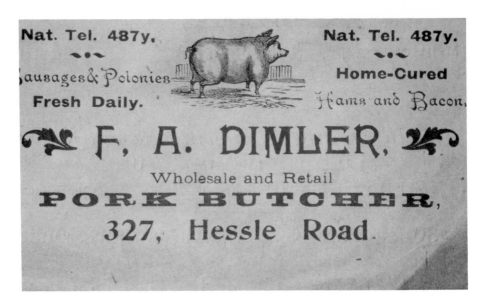

Nat. Tel. 487y.    Nat. Tel. 487y.

Sausages & Polonies    Home-Cured

Fresh Daily.    Hams and Bacon.

# F, A. DIMLER,

Wholesale and Retail

## PORK BUTCHER,

### 327, Hessle Road.

*The pig taboo was stronger at sea than in the fishing community. There were various pork butcher shops along Hessle Road. The above advertisement is from a 1913 charity concert programme for three lost Hull trawlers. Below is a picture of old curly-tail in the flesh (at Burdale, Yorkshire Wolds). Apparently, there was a Walker's Pig Farm in Dairycoates near the old Hessle Road level-crossing. Ursula Wright came from a posh family in English Street and, before the First World War, they often bought a whole pig from a local farmer. She described how "everything was used except the squeak".*
Copyright Alec Gill.

set sail the next day. Again, we have another instance whereby the powerful 'never-turn-back' rule is stood on its head by the stronger pig taboo. Radford (1974) reported the tail of a Scottish vessel which also turned back after being confronted by a similar problem. A young prankster threw a sow's tail aboard a fishing boat as it sailed out of Buckhaven harbour. The ship "instantly turned back and the crewmen refused to sail until the next day" (p.265).

The second Hull trawling story is almost identical, but the skipper did not turn back to port. As the *Macbeth* (H.113) steamed off down the Humber in 1948, skipper Ben Henry glanced from the bridge as the deckhands cleared the ship's stores from the open deck. One of the men's jobs was to unleash the bale of hides. These were used to make the covers water-tight when the 'hatches were battened down'. And to protect the trawl net from the jagged rocks when dragged along the seabed. But Skipper Henry's eagle-eye spotted a particular hide which caused his blood to boil. John Crimlis describes how "he went daft, used lots of foul language and ordered the bewildered deckhands to throw the pigskin overboard". After things calmed down, the 1938-built *Macbeth* continued her voyage to the White Sea.

There are other yarns, but the third and final porky tale is told by John Evans who wrote to me (8 Mar. 90). This incident is perhaps best told by an extract from his letter:

*"I was mate of the **James Barrie** [H.15] with skipper Bernard Stipetic –now deceased. Every time I saw a piece of pork come out of the fish room for dinner I would say 'Here comes some bad luck'. One day [c.1960] we had just put a new trawl on and, lo and behold, up came a back leg of pork out of the fish room. I cursed and swore. Bernard said, 'I'll cure you of this superstition'. He cut off the grunter's tail and tied it to the headline of the trawl and we shot away. We had not been towing fifteen minutes, when BANG, BANG – both warps parted [loosing thousands of pounds worth of valuable gear snagged on the rocks]. After that, pork was never allowed on board the **James Barrie** again".*

This attitude toward grunter has also been reported in Brixham — home of the earliest smack owners who settled in Hull during the 1840s. Opie & Tatem (1989) told how Devonshire fishermen never carried pork to sea (p.307). This Brixham-pig link provides a useful clue as to why Hull's fishing families were so bound by superstition — a point for later discussion (Ch. 32).

No one I have interviewed knows how or why this 'grunting animal' is so critical to Hull trawlermen. Nor is it clear whether this link is out of fear or favour. I do not know either. But I have had lots of fun trying to sort this one out. The research has led into some dark and mysterious back-waters. Pigs are certainly amazing creatures who have entwined themselves deep within the human psyche. The picture built up from the literature can be described as fairly contradictory. As we saw earlier with the chequered history of the cat — so it is with parger-warger. In Pagan times it was revered, in Christian reviled.

Pagans praised the pig from Iceland to the Indus. The pre-historic ancestor of the farm-yard pig was, naturally, the wild boar. These two names are used here inter-changeably. In an earlier publication, I described the Pagan boar in terms of Frazer's (1922) corn-spirits (Gill, 1991, p.81). I still stand by this theory, but have since found that the boar/pig was much more central to the whole of the Celtic belief system than first realised. Gratitude goes to anthropologist Dr. Dennis Duerden of Hull University who kindly lent a copy of the Anne Ross (1974) book *Pagan Celtic Britain*. She showed that "the boar is, without doubt, the cult animal *par excellence* of the Celts...which has the greatest representational popularity, and one which is used in a wide variety of contexts" (p.390). Ross described how boar symbols are found throughout the Celtic world on helmets, shields, cauldrons, coins, banners, altars, and in the graves of powerful tribal chieftains. This popular animal also had a protective 'talismanic significance' in military warfare. This divine swine is a cult hero in Irish and Welsh mythology. Anne Ross concluded that the immortal pig "contained all the passions of the Celtic peoples — hunting, feasting, fighting and procreation (it is a symbol of sexual fertility — p.404). As Christianity grew in strength, so the boar's popularity rapidly diminished throughout Europe. But old curly-tail craftily foraged his way into British folklore. And our coastal fishermen kept porker alive in their enigmatic superstitions. Later in this book, I will argue that the pig/boar is the totem animal of the fishing families (Ch. 26 & 32).

The Holy Bible has few, if any, good things to say about the swine. The idols of a dying religion are usually despised, destroyed and denigrated by other in-coming religions. The Jews were the first pig-bashers. A few extracts from the Old Testament will suffice: Leviticus instructed the children of Israel, "You must not eat their [swine] meat or touch their carcasses, they are unclean for you" (11:7). Isaiah condemned those who "eat swines' flesh" (65:4; 66:17). And Proverbs stated, "As a jewel of gold in a swine's snout, so is a fair woman who is without discretion" (11:22) — this also takes a swipe at women. When the Israelites conquered Canaan, they found that the native inhabitants offered swine "as a sacrifice in idolatrous worship" (Encyclopædia Judaica, 1971, p.506) — and stamped it out.

The medical argument, sometimes put forward to explain this anti-pork view, is obviously strong. Parasitic tapeworm can infect under-cooked ham (shoulder). Once in the human gut, it can grow over three feet long. Even today there is no direct treatment for cysticercosis. Untreated, the patient goes mad.

The Christian New Testament has at least two references to pigs. Jesus told his followers not to "cast ye your pearls before swine, lest they trample them under their feet" (Matthew 7:6). But the most direct biblical link between grunter and mariner comes from the story of the Gadarene Swine. Jesus had just stepped ashore in Gadarene when a mad man with an 'unclean spirit' fell to his knees before Him. The man was possessed by a legion of demons. Christ cast them into 2000 pigs on a nearby mountain side. Then "the herd ran violently down a steep place into the sea and were choked in the sea" (Mark 5:1-20). So here is a clear link between pigs and drowning. Audiences have suggested to me that trawlermen who wish to avoid drowning, therefore, avoid pig.

There seems no easy way to draw together the diverse and patchy evidence related to pigs. The mystical and biblical views conflict wildly. I doubt if Hull trawlermen subscribed much to the anti-pig views of the Jews and Christians. Had they been avid Bible followers, then why did they have taboos related to rabbits, cats, and rats when there are very few references to any of these animals in the holy book (Metzger, 1962)? On the other hand, the New Testament banished goats to the Fires of Hell (Matthew 25:31-41), but this old hairy-whiskers does not appear at all in any trawling taboo.

I have already written extensively about skipper 'Mad' Rilatt and his suicidal World War One antics (Gill, 1991, Ch.2). He swam against the tide in almost every aspect of his life. Not surprisingly he was also out of step with this taboo. Instead of avoiding grunter, he embraced him as a lucky mascot. In addition to his lucky hog-shaped silver match-stick holder (which 'protected' him through both world wars), he even had a bigger model of a sow which he took to sea. His son Ted confided that Mad broke it off a car bonnet — perhaps a mascot-type figure. Anyway, he took it to sea for years on whatever trawler he had under his command. Then one day it was stolen from the wheelhouse. Much to Mad's anger, it was never found. The Rilatt family still suspect that it was taken by a rival skipper called, appropriately, Charlie Hogg.

**Chapter 18**

## 'FOUR-FOOTED BEASTIES'

NURSERY RHYME: *White Rabbit, White Rabbit,*
*Give me Good Luck*
*If you don't*
*I'll stamp my foot.*

### WHITE RABBITS

We left the grunter section with Mad Rilatt swearing and stamping at another skipper for stealing his lucky swine mascot. But when it came to rabbits Mad was not so brave. He bluntly refused to say this word. Instead, he cursingly called them Bob-tailed Bastards or Buck-tailed Bastards. Ted Rilatt tells how his dad had such an aversion that he would do anything to avoid this harmless creature.

The fact that both rabbit and hare are taboo names has been researched by Opie & Tatem (1989). In the late 13th century they were referred to as "the animals that no one dare name"; in 1602 the advice was "do not utter the name of the Hare or such uncouth things, for that proves ominous for fishermen"; Flamborough fishermen in 1875 "had a great fear if rabbits were spoken of" —and they still use the substitute word Jacko [for Jack Rabbit, I suppose]; in 1919 other alternatives for Rabbit were "those hairy things" or "one of them furry things" [both confirmed by Hull trawlermen in the 1990s]; and, in 1965, Banff fishermen in Buckie refer to Rabbit Island [in the Kyle of Tongue] as "Gentleman's Island" to avoid using the unlucky word (pp. 192-93).

In some parts of Scotland, I am told, rabbit is called Mappy. Two more Hull alternatives are 'That animal with long ears' and 'Bunny'. One interviewee is of the opinion that Grimsby skippers are much more sensitive about this taboo than Yorkie crewmen (who are more afraid of pig). Indeed, it was Ron 'Sweat' Haines' experience that if the word 'pig' was uttered, it was counter-acted by repeatedly saying 'Bunny Rabbits, Bunny Rabbits' to avert bad luck. Mischievous Hull skippers, therefore, called up their rivals on the GY-boats and contrived a conversation about "rabbit-pie". The Grimmies angrily shouted back over the airwaves, "Don't say that word! I've got me cod-end down!".

Arthur Chambers is researching the World War Two trawlers and he passed on a bunny story from one of his correspondents. Although the majority of the war-time crews were fishermen, civvies — ignorant of seafaring ways — also served on the mine-sweeping trawlers. One such wireless operator decided to do the crew a favour by enriching the ship's menu with a brace of rabbits. The RNR skipper was quietly on the bridge one evening when a commotion suddenly erupted in the fo'c'sle. He sent an officer to investigate. When he heard there were Long-ears on board, he diplomatically called in his sparks and

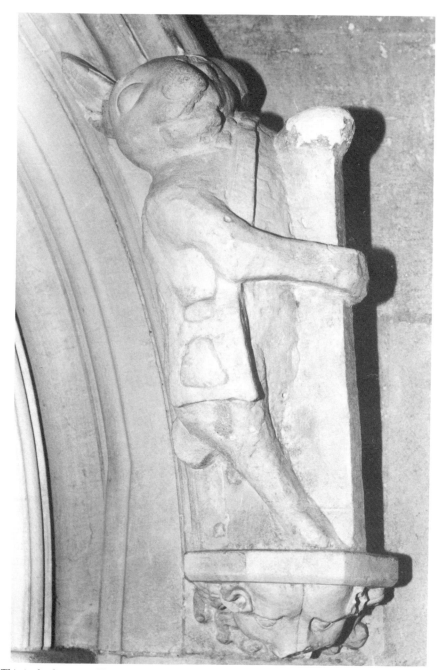

*This is the famous rabbit in St. Mary's Church, Beverley. It is said to have been the inspiration behind Lewis Carroll's White Rabbit in 'Alice in Wonderland'. The rabbit's importance in folk magic is as a symbol of fertility – associated with the Goddess of Spring called Eastre. The rabbit (or hare) was her familiar. The cockleshell on the satchel of the St. Mary's rabbit suggests that he is on a pilgrimage. Note the pig's head underneath the base of the statue – yet more animal magic (Ch. 18).*
Copyright Alec Gill.

"persuaded him to drop the rabbits overboard. That done, peace was restored".

I have come across no community tales about rabbits. Apart, that is, from Dick Jackson whose father had almost thirty furry creatures. These were kept in a brick hut with a stove on an allotment. But no mention of any superstition — these creatures were to feed the Jackson family.

There are lots of tales in the literature to the effect that "if a rabbit or hare crosses the path of a fisherman, he will not sail that day" (Radford, 1974, p.181) — but no Hessle Roader has mentioned this type of incident. Still on the local, shore-based level, St. Mary's Church at Beverley provides a marvellous combination of two tabooed animals in one statue. Inside is a splendid sculpture of a White Rabbit. Apparently, this particular one is said to have impressed Lewis Carroll who included a white rabbit in *Alice in Wonderland*. But what is fascinating is that this rabbit is stood on the head of a pig. I could not believe my eyes when I saw them both together. St. Mary's was built around 1330/40 when, no doubt, the animal symbolism was more readily understood than it is today. Fishermen of that period would certainly have known that the rabbit or hare was a witches' familiar — her "soft-footed servant" (Lehane, 1984, p.100); and that this animal is involved in divination of future events.

When the Romans fought Boadicea she released a hare from her cloak (Farrar, 1987, p.192). The direction it dashed was seen by the Britons as a forecast of how to conduct their battle — is this why the Romans won? Rabbits, hares and divination will pop up again later (Ch. 22). We now dart from bob-tail to long-tail.

## LONG-TAILS

One of the most universally-known animal maritime superstitions is: "rats desert a doomed ship". This was popular amongst Hull trawlermen too. The common alternative name widely used throughout the port is Long-tail. Some used the expression, "There goes a longy". A Radio Humberside listener mentioned that, "If you said the word 'rat', you got a dirty look at home" (Mar. 1990). A modern anecdote illustrates that even alternatives can become taboo words themselves. Edith Smith tells of her son Neil who sails aboard the Marr trawlers (1993). He points out that crewmen nowadays refuse to utter either the word Rat or Long-tail. Instead, they are called Bradfords. This name is not new, but its origin is a mystery. Tom Magee said the term Bradford Lads (which he used for rats) might be to do with rugby, and that this expression was in use before the last war.

Although Longies are condemned as unhygienic vermin and are often despised, they are nevertheless a lucky omen if spotted aboard a trawler — at least it means the ship will not sink. Ships' runner Alf Stockdale of Boyd Line explains that, "If you have a rat on board, the ship won't sink. But if seen deserting, the ship never came back. That's been proved time and time again". A practical account for why a rat leaves a sinking ship is that "these creatures hate to be wet, and if a vessel is beginning to leak — the first sign of disaster — they will go looking for new quarters" (Haining, 1979, p.151). A more mystical view, however, holds that rats "were anciently associated with the souls of men, and consequently they were regarded as ominous creatures, having foreknowledge of what is to come" (Radford, 1974, p.279).

## SEA-DOGS

'Dog' spelt backwards is 'God' — which might be why this word is another trawling taboo. What I do not know is if there was ever an alternative word which the trawlermen used. Was it 'waggy-tail'? 'Man's best friend' is both a good and bad omen at sea.

For many years Hull skipper Big Chris had a large black spaniel aboard the *Bayflower* (H.487). In the early 1930s he picked it up as a pup at a Norwegian port. Because of British quarantine restrictions, Chris was never allowed to bring him ashore at Hull. Consequently, the spaniel grew up and lived for several years aboard the 396-ton trawler. Big Chris said, "I'd never part with him for a fortune because he is the luckiest mascot I've ever taken to sea" (Willis, 1937, p.52).

There are some who believe it is unlucky to take a dog to sea. But I have been given lots of photographs, especially of trawlermen in the Royal Navy during the Second World War, which show a dog being held up as the ship's talisman. The *Lord Lloyd* (H.508 — FY.157), for example, had a little mongrel terrier on board — and this trawler survived the war. But an unlucky tale of a dog is associated with the sinking of the *Kingston Turquoise* (H.50). Her loss in 1965 brought about the death of the practical joker nicknamed Dillinger (Gill, 1991, Ch. 14). The 205-ft. trawler struck a tiny uncharted reef off the Orkneys on 25 January. After helping to launch the life-boats and seeing the rest of the crew safely off the distressed trawler, dare-devil Dill suddenly went back toward the wheel-house. We will never know why he did not save his own skin; but I believe he impulsively dashed back to save his pet dog *Lassie*. Mavis Wegg, a cousin of his, points out that perhaps the reason he died was because he 'turned back' and broke his own good luck. Only Dillinger and his dog were lost with the sinking of the *Turquoise*.

Perhaps the main reason why dogs feature in folk lore is because it is said they can detect or foresee the approach of Death.

# Chapter 20

## PISCES

PROVERB: *The best fish swim near the bottom.*

In the book *Superstitions of Sailors* the point is made that "every creature on land has its counterpart in the sea... Many fish are named after land animals, as: the sea-dog, the sea-sow, the sea-cat" (Rappoport, 1930, p.157). He then develops this argument to show how legends arose about "mermen and mermaids" (p.164).

It was inevitable that over the centuries fishermen would dream up many myths, legends and superstitions around fish. Pisces is a pair of parallel fish pointing in opposite directions, "symbolising spiritual and temporal power, the upper and lower worlds, past and future...the ending of one cycle and the beginning of another" (Dunnigan, 1987, p.346). Fish, the last sign of the Zodiac, are the first form of life on Earth — according to both the Bible and Science.

In past times and in some cultures, fish worship was not uncommon. In the Old Testament the worshipping of fish was forbidden (Deuteronomy 6:18). In the New, the symbol of Jesus is the fish. And many of his disciples were fishermen who became 'fishers of men'. The feeding of the five thousand was done with five loaves and two fishes. These are said to have been haddock and the 'thumb-print' found on the side of this species is claimed to be that of Christ's. In both Christian and Jewish festivities, fish is a sacred dish. And every Good Friday fish is the only flesh which Christians traditionally eat — as they remember the crucifixion of the King of Kings.

There are three Royal Fish which, if caught near the British coast, are the property of the Crown: sturgeon, whale (not a fish, but a mammal), and porpoise. The friendly porpoise must never be harmed. When they swim around a trawler, it is a good omen for the voyage. Their playful behaviour foretells the weather ahead. If they swim swiftly southward, a gale is due, if they dart wildly during a storm, calm weather will follow, if they are seen to travel quickly northward, it is a sure sign of calm seas. An interesting aside is that the origin of the word 'porpoise' is a further example of an animal correspondence and takes us back to our old friend Grunter. This name is a combination of two Latin words *Pocus* for pig and *Pisces* for fish. In other words, it is a pig-fish — perhaps because both have a blunt snout. It might be that this favourable view of the pig-fish springs from the fishermen's affinity with its land-based equivalent (Ch. 18).

Fish divide into lucky or unlucky types within trawling folklore. The first fish caught foretold how good or bad the rest of the trip would be. A female boded well for the voyage. On some boats, the first fish was always thrown back into the sea (Frazer, 1922, p.528). But on the old herring drifters, the first fish was nailed to the mast as a thanks offering and to ensure that others would follow. The catch must not be counted; if they were no more would be caught that day. We saw in an earlier section how neither the skipper nor mate discussed the quantity of fish on board (Ch. 11).

The luckiest of all species is the fiddle fish. *The Times* national newspaper (5 Aug. 49) reported that for the first time in ten years, a fiddle fish had been caught by the Fleetwood-based trawler *Jamaica* (LO.180 — formerly H.216). The article mentioned, "The fish was at once slung over the stern by the crew for towing in the traditional way". This meant it was dragged behind the trawler until it fell to pieces. The fiddle fish must never be eaten. There are arguments about the direction in which a fish should be eaten. Some say from the head to the tail so that other fish in the seas will head toward the trawler. But mackerel, herring, and pilchards must be eaten from the tail to the head so that the main shoal will not turn tail and swim away from the drift nets. A Lord Line bosun believed, "Crab must never be eaten.

*Hull trawlermen had a love-hate relationship with the fish they caught. One of the most despised species was the oarkettle – a type of shark. This rare, fuzzy 1934 picture shows two men attacking a helpless creature strung up in the rigging by its tail. The man on deck has a large spanner just about (or pretending) to hit the oarkettle's skull. The chap above is waving a large knife, ready to cut its tail off. The poor creature was then doomed to swim around in an endless circle until it died.*
Courtesy John Crimlis.

They are dead fishermen, and so it would be like eating a lost friend".

The most feared of all fish was the shark —the aquatic vulture. If sharks followed a trawler, especially in a group of three, the fear was that a death will soon occur on board. The dark shark has an acute sense of smell for blood. It even detected if there was an injured man on the vessel — say, someone who lost an arm in the winch gear. News that hungry shark were following the ship was usually kept from a sick trawlerman — so as not to scare him to death. Superstition, not unnaturally, sees the sinister shark as an omen of death.

Peter Haining (1979), in a chapter called *Peril at sea*, reviewed a wide range of seafaring superstitions. Talking about fishermen overall, he stated "the mention of pigs, hares and rabbits is considered unlucky. If a man inadvertently mentions one of these creatures he and the crew members must grab hold of the nearest iron implement and shout 'COLD IRON!'" (p.157). Just as land-lubbers might 'Touch Wood', so Hull trawlermen reach for cold iron as a protective object against evil. Objects, like animals, also have magic.

# PART FOUR
## OBJECTS

## Chapter 21
## HOME, SWEET HOME

SONG: *Keep the home fires burning,*
*While your hearts are yearning.*
(Lena Ford)

Part Four brings together a range of inanimate objects. We begin with household items and then food in the kitchen; colour, time and number also fall into this mixed bag, before we look at objects afloat.

The home is adorned with superstitious objects and items. Even the front-door keys jangle with magic. It is an ill-omen if they are dropped; but bad luck is averted by immediately standing on them before they are picked up. Visitors must leave by the same door they enter. Otherwise, they take the luck of the house with them. When I went to interview top skipper Harold Hall about the time he sneaked his wife aboard a trawler (Ch. 6), he stressed the point that he was not superstitious at all (indeed, he had become a Catholic). Nevertheless, when the time came for me to leave, I was not allowed to exit the house other than by the door I had entered. The origin of this is probably from the occult world where rituals were performed within a magic circle. Illustrations of this ancient power is shown in the circles of stone at Stonehenge, Avebury, and elsewhere in the Celtic world. And the twelve houses of the Zodiac are usually drawn in a circle. The symbolic door of some sacred circles is represented by a broom-stick. Anyone allowed into this hallowed place must leave by the same way they enter — otherwise the magic of the circle is broken.

George and Maureen Flitton recall that "if ever someone went out of the house and were forced to return, they had to sit down and count to ten in order to break their journey" (3/84). Children were punished if they swung on a door. The explanation is that "this blew up a gale for those at sea". Cordelia Jones remembers that "if stood by a door chatting, you must never idly swing it".

Crossing on the stairs is strictly forbidden. Lizzie Ramshaw of Division Road believed that if two people are going up the stairs and the one in front tripped, this was a sign of a wedding. Up in the bedroom, there is a superstitious tip for those who cannot sleep. To avoid night-mares, sleep with the open end of the pillow case pointing out of the bed. This enables horrid dreams to find an easy release.

'Shoes on a table' kicked off many a row. Cordelia Jones' taboo-ridden granny never put footwear (or a hat) on a bed, and especially not shoes on a table. She also stipulated that shoes must never be stored higher than one's own height. It is bad luck to place them on a high shelf. I was told a story at the Hessle Afternoon Townswomen's Guild of a man who absent-mindedly placed a pair of new shoes on the table after his return from the shops. When he realised, he quickly placed them on the floor, stood in front of them and jumped over them backwards to avert the bad luck which would follow this serious mistake. I have not traced the origin of this shoe taboo. Apart from being unlucky, the literature claimed that shoes-on-table will result in a quarrel (Opie & Tatem, 1989, p.350).

A picture falling off the wall is associated with death — more so if a portrait falls in the dead of the night. The person featured will be the one who will die. Should there be three people in the picture, the one in the middle will be the first victim — no mention is made if an even number of people. Incidents of this kind are often related to 'having a premonition' or 'foreboding about the future' (Ch. 31). This happened in February 1925 prior to the mysterious sinking of *Field Marshal Robertson* (H.104) on her return from Iceland. "Almost everyone said they had a premonition — pictures dropped off the wall, lamps broke — or they had a vision of their loved ones" (A. W. Anlaby, *Fishing Years* No. 2, Mar. 89, p.20).

A universal belief is that seven years bad luck will befall anyone who breaks a mirror. Such a long-term curse reflects the high degree of importance given to the looking-glass — again we enter the world of magic for an explanation. The seven-year punishment for this ill-deed comes from the old "anatomical myth that the human body underwent a complete physical renewal every seven years ... it was only at the end of this period that bad luck could be eradicated from our system" (Blackcat, 1988, p.196). Protection of the sacred mirror was vital. This was dramatically illustrated at No. 76 Manchester Street in the Taylor household whenever a thunderstorm loomed overhead. Young Cordelia, brought up by her strict gran, said "she was like a whirl-wind —dashing from room to room quickly covering over every mirror. For the big one we used a bed sheet". But the young grand-daughter did not always go along with gran's mirror magic. Cordelia was told, "If you stare into a mirror long enough, the Devil will appear and stare back at you!". As a defiant girl, she secretly decided to try this one out. Alone in the house, Cordelia sat before a mirror and stared and stared as the moments ticked away. Would Satan appear? — "I almost scared myself to death!"

Mirrors were also covered in a room where someone was at death's door. It was believed that a dying person's weakened soul — hovering between life and death — would be unable to return to the body should it catch sight of itself in a mirror. Equally, after the death, "mirrors were veiled, or turned to the wall, for fear that the soul might become entangled in the reflection" and not ascend to heaven (Reader's Digest, 1977, p.89). In olden days, mirrors were believed to deflect the harmful rays of the Evil Eye. Furthermore, they were used in the practice of divination (Catoptromancy) by seers or scryers. The ancient Greeks placed a mirror in water. Today, we speak about 'gazing into a crystal ball'. Scrying was forbidden by the established church. A New Testament quote which condemned this form of prophesy is "for now we see through a glass darkly" (1 Corinthians 13:9-12). In 1649 a woman was executed at Salisbury because "she did tell fortunes, and showed people visions in a glasse, and that a maid saw the devil with her" (Opie & Tatem, 1989, p.252). It seems that ordinary people's faith in mirror magic is not completely shattered — and fragments survive today disguised as superstition.

From mirror magic we are drawn into fire lore. The natural heart of the

*Fire is one of the four elements. Its wild movement, colour, warmth and energy meant it was guaranteed a place in the world of magic. Dancing flames captivate the human mind. Fire spirits were easy to imagine. Vesta was the Goddess of Fire in ancient Rome. The embers, sparks and loud cracks were messages from the gods. Many Hessle Road women sat by their kitchen range – after a busy day – on the look out for signs of the future. One such 'fire watcher' was Lizzie Ramshaw: seen here in the leafy yard of her Division Road home – adjusting her pillow (c.1928).*
Courtesy Jean Wilson.

traditional home is the fire place. A kitchen range literally sparked off endless superstitious omens. Some women watched eagerly whenever a cinder shot out of the grate — each had a message (a sign from the fire gods?). A round-shaped spark was a cradle and indicated that a baby was due. A long oblong warned of the opposite — death. If this coffin-like spark was silent, that doubly confirmed a funeral was nigh. A square shape meant a letter. If it came with a loud crack, a fortune would follow. Some Hessle Road women claimed to make out the shape of a ship in the glowing spark. The woman clapped or wafted her hands over the cinder and began to slowly count. Depending on how long the fanned ember lasted, indicated the number of days before the news came through of a trawler lost at sea. This home-spun divination by fire (pyromancy) was not uncommon in Britain (Opie & Tatem, 1989, pp.152-154). Elizabeth Ramshaw — 'Our Lizzie' — at No. 9 Whitfield Avenue, Division Road, was a keen fire witch. Twenty-three years a widow, she spent most evenings, after her busy working day, in her low nursing chair in front of the grate. She stared into the fire and sometimes suddenly yelled out to her daughter Jean who dashed from the kitchen.

"Look! Look! It's a man's face". Sceptical Jean protested that she could not see a thing. Lizzie grabbed the poker and began to point, "See! There's his eyes and nose. He has a beard, there's his hair. It looks like Mister So-and-So. And he is going to visit". Jean added, "And more often than not, he did call by in the next few days". At other times, Lizzie saw the face of her deceased William. Black flakes of soot waving on the grate meant 'a stranger on the bar' — this means an unknown person would visit soon. If the Ramshaw's fire was roaring away brightly with a bluish tinge, "It's frosty out today" commented Lizzie; but in some households this meant a sign of money to come. Geoff Wilkinson recalls from his boyhood days, "You could always tell a woman who sat by her fire for ages — she had corned-beef (blotchy) legs".

Even boring domestic chores were riddled with signs of good or bad luck ahead. The golden rule when stitching a small tear or a button on a dress, was not to do so while wearing it: "You'll sew bad luck into your back". One lady described it as, "Sewing sorrow to your back".

We have seen the washing taboo on sailing day (Ch. 1), but even hanging things on a line had its do's and don'ts. Net-braiding forewoman Lil Walheim strongly felt that "three sheets hung out together were a sure sign of death". An elderly chap once explained that in the days of sailing smacks, if a storm suddenly whipped up and you had three sails (sheets) in the rigging, then the ship was in danger of being blown over. Thus, the mariner's warning is to avoid "three sheets to the wind"; and perhaps the women ashore imitated this because it had links with death at sea — sympathetic magic again. A staggering drunk is also described as being 'three sheets to the wind' — perhaps because he reels around like a ship in a storm. Another sheet-cum-death omen concerns the family bedding. Many a cold shiver shot down the spine when a diamond-shaped crease was spotted in the middle of a sheet. To find this cursed message caused worry in many a Hessle Road household. Doris Gerrard associated this omen with the loss of her husband Joseph. He had just taken his first trip on a Hull trawler since serving on the mine-sweepers during the Second World War.

He managed to get a job aboard the *Kingston Pearl* (H.542). On 16 February 1946 she was homeward bound from the northern Norwegian fishing grounds when "this terrific sea hit us and laid us over on our port side ... Joe had just left the bridge as the sea struck and didn't have a chance" (J. Austwick, *Fishing Years*, No. 3, Oct. 89, p.11). Joseph's son Bernard remembers "that for several weeks after losing dad, we kept finding diamond shapes in bed-linen, table-clothes and tea-towels".

Clothes put on inside out must not be changed or "you'll change your luck too". Sometimes, however, if a series of things went wrong in the kitchen a woman deliberately took off her pinny (apron) and put it back on inside out to change her run of bad luck. Stephen Stipetic, who grew up in a fishing family down West Dock Avenue, said "if a young girl was scrubbing the floor, her mother told her not to get her apron wet or she'd marry a drunkard".

Future relationships with the opposite sex were also forecast by the kitchen cutlery. If two teaspoons end up in a cup, this is a sign of a wedding. Even the dropping of cutlery tells who is about to visit the house. A dropped knife tells of a male visitor; a fork means a woman will call, and a spoon means a baby is due. The strongest cutlery taboo is two crossed knives. This, the symbol of two crossed swords, foretells an angry quarrel in the home. Jim Anderson takes this one step further and says: "crossed knives means a death". If ever two knives are found crossed, the rule is to "always remove the bottom one first" — then, the dispute is avoided. Cordelia Jones was always told "never leave a knife or fork on a plate with a spoon in the middle". The childhood memories of Stan and Evelyn Futty are that "if a thunder-storm suddenly broke out when the table was set, we were told to quickly hide away all the cutlery to prevent lightning striking indoors" — this is similar to the mirror drama we saw earlier.

Should a sharp knife or any object (like scissors or a broach) be given as a gift, then a coin was given in exchange "so as not to cut the friendship" (Rilatt family). In his authorative tome *The Golden Bough*, James Frazer (1922) demonstrated that in primitive tribes throughout the world any sharp weapon is surrounded by taboo. After a death in the house, great care was taken with knives for fear of stabbing "the soul of the dead" (p.227). Another explanation comes from the practice of witchcraft. In sacred rituals knives with black and white handles were used in certain ceremonies. During the witch-hunts, these ceremonial implements were 'hidden' by mixing them in with the kitchen utensils. Therefore, extra "care was taken in handling any knife in case it was a magic one" (Jo de Gournai). Apparently, "in 1646, the sticking of knives across [is the] mark of witches" (Opie & Tatem, 1989, p.218).

## Chapter 22

## FOOD MAGIC

TABOO: *Don't throw bread on the fire*
*– you'll feed the Devil.*

### 'STAFF OF LIFE'

Bread featured at critical times such as when the family moved house. Net-braider Freda Fee told that before they flitted from the Boulevard, friendly neighbours gave them a piece of bread, wood and coal. They insisted, "Here, take these for luck in your new house". These are symbolic objects, with bread to fend off hunger and coal for warmth. I am not too sure about wood, but in folklore the 'wood spirits' are of paramount importance — thus we 'touch wood'.

Freda's mother, Lil Walheim, told her children never to sit on a table or "you'll want for dough" — a reference to bread-making, not money-making. One lady who lived in the community, not involved with trawling, commented that "when we cut a loaf in our house it was turned over on the bread-board. But not in a fishing family or you'd turn a ship over at sea". This physical up ending of the loaf is more mimic magic whereby the action mirrors a trawler's stern pointing skywards as it plunged beneath the waves. Bread magic is reported elsewhere by Opie & Tatem (1989). They mentioned that in the North of England (1866) "along the coast, they say, that for every loaf turned upside down a ship will be wrecked" (p.39). But bread also acts as a *protection* for a trawlerman going to sea.

Albert Gerrard's wife Maria always wrapped the crust of a loaf in newspaper and placed it carefully at the bottom of his seabag on sailing day. Albert was told to bring it back and this was replaced by a new slice for the next trip. The magical protection, apparently, worked, for Albert was never lost at sea. Academic literature also sheds some light on this ritual. Radford (1974) stated that "sailors formerly took a hot-cross bun on their voyages to prevent shipwreck...The same protective and healing powers were ascribed to bread baked on Good Friday or on Christmas Day" (p.200). This practice echoes something mentioned by the late Lord Mayor of Hull Louis Pearlman. He grew up in the community and at Jewish Passover "people knocked at our door and asked for a piece of Passover Bread. It was believed to be lucky".

### SPILT SALT

A key ingredient in baking bread is a pinch of salt. This too has magic properties. A universal belief is that spilt salt must be thrown over the left shoulder. Hessle Roaders added a few local variations. It is unlucky to pass salt from one person to another at sea: "Pass salt, pass sorrow". A young wireless sparks did this once and was angrily told, "Put it down on the table!!" The word 'salt' is taboo aboard ship. Mike Dash (Bristol) said that "you must never mention this word on any boat or the sea might hear you and want its own back" (1/93). *Reader's Digest* (1977) claimed that fishermen have a long-winded alternative for salt: "some of that white stuff...not the stuff you put in your tea" (p.73).

John Nicholson (1890) reported an old East Riding expression that "for every grain of salt spilt a tear will be shed" (p.43). The link here is that there is salt in our tears (and in sea water). In the U.S.A. "every grain spilt means a day of sorrow" (Waring, 1978, p.199). Some Hessle Road sayings are "never lend salt, rather give it away" and "if you spill salt it means sorrow, but spilt sugar implies joy". There are various explanations about salt magic. The practical-minded claim that salt was once a precious commodity which must not be wasted — and so it became unlucky to spill it. This logic soon breaks down when the transgressor is seen wasting even more by flinging it over the left shoulder.

A more mystical account brings us face to face with the Devil. Salt is an incorruptible element. Old Nick hates whatever he cannot corrupt. And, as Satan always sits on our left (sinister) shoulder, so we throw salt in his eyes. If east-coast Scottish fishermen have a spell of bad luck, Anson (1932) said, "a pinch of salt is thrown after the skipper and his crew when they leave home ... and even into the boat itself" (p.59). This is to stop the Devil dogging their tracks or cursing their nets. I recently heard an expression from a Scottish lady whose husband worked aboard the Hull trawlers: "It's unlucky to throw fresh water on a salt-water man".


## *EGG-SHELLS AND WITCHES*

'Egg' like 'salt', is another taboo word aboard fishing boats. Its alternative (or nickname) is 'roundabout' or 'round one'. Eggs were forbidden on many fishing vessels around the British coast. In 1885 it was reported that "eggs are supposed to cause contrary winds and there are fishermen that would not allow a single one on board" (Opie & Tatem, 1989, p.134). And, in Hull, the trawler owners did not provide eggs for their crews. What must be quickly added, however, is that this was more out of a penny-pinching motive than a respect for a time-honoured superstition. Some crewmen took their own. They gave a half-dozen to the cook who fried them as a special treat during the course of the voyage. After the Second World War, John Crimlis mentioned, a man could buy a few eggs from the ship's bond. At sea or ashore, "you were really lucky if ever you got an egg with a double yoke".

The strongest evidence of egg magic comes not from trawlermen this time, but stories in the community. In Anson's (1932) chapter about 'Folk-lore and Superstitions' there is only one reference to Hull — and this concerns food. He stated, "at Hull and Hartlepool it was formerly customary when a fisherman's child was first taken to visit a neighbour to give it a piece of bread and an egg" (p.34). No one has ever mentioned this tradition to me. Nevertheless, children and eggs have strong links in Hessle Road homes. Kids were firmly told to smash up the empty shells after eating a boiled egg. One mother always crushed her daughter's left-over egg shell saying, "There you are, now the witches can't sail in them". This witch clue about the origin of the taboo was confirmed later at a talk to the Hull Brave's Guild. Someone in the audience cited the opening lines of a childhood rhyme which linked eggs with sailors. An appeal on Peter Adamson's Radio Humberside 'Soap Box' programme soon provided all the verses from listener Flora Franks. She kindly photocopied the poem by Elizabeth Fleming (1934) called *Egg-shells*. It goes:

> *Oh, never leave your egg-shells unbroken in the cup;*
> *Think of us poor sailor-men and always smash them up,*
> *For witches come and find them and sail away to sea,*
> *And make a lot of misery for mariners like me.*

> *They take them to the sea-shore and set them on the tide –*
> *A broom-stick for a paddle is all they have to guide –*
> *And off they go to China or round the ports of Spain,*
> *To try and keep our sailing ships from coming home again.*

> *They call up all the tempests from Davy Jones's store,*
> *And blow us into waters where we haven't been before;*
> *And when the masts are falling in splinters on the wrecks,*
> *The witches climb the rigging and dance upon the decks.*

> *So never leave your egg-shells unbroken in the cup;*
> *Think of us poor sailor-men and always smash them up;*
> *For witches come and find them and sail away to sea,*
> *And make a lot of misery for mariners like me.*

The tiny egg has been the centre of magic since creation. The Roman Pliny (77 AD) wrote about the fear associated with eggs: "there is no one...who does not dread being spell-bound by means of evil imprecations; and hence the practice, after eating eggs or snails, of immediately breaking shells or piercing them with a spoon" (Opie & Tatem, 1989, p.135). Practically all religions adopt the egg as a key symbol. A caller on Radio Humberside suggested "the egg depicts the rolling away of the stone from the tomb of Christ" (Apr. 1990). Others claim it represents the resurrection. And, indeed, eggs are given to children on Easter Monday — a day central to the Christian calendar. But the Bible itself has few references to eggs.

In the world of superstition, the rich symbolism of the egg comes more from Pagan roots where the egg is associated with fertility. If we return again to Easter Eggs, it take minimal research to find that Eastre is the Pagan Goddess of Spring and Fertility ('oestrum' being Latin for "violent sexual desire"; and 'estrogen' being a female sex hormone). The appearance of the Easter Bunny is no mere chance at this seasonal event (Ch. 19). Eastre's animal familiar is a magic hare which laid brightly-coloured eggs. Every Spring, village children throughout Europe searched for eggs which had been dyed various colours. This is why the 'Eastre' Eggs we give children today are wrapped in glistening silver paper.

From this magic symbolism came scores of egg games played every Spring: egg-rolling, egg-tossing, and egg-and-spoon races. But the sacred Pagan egg was soon scorned as the Church spread its influence into the Dark Ages. Hares were despised as the thieving familiars of wicked witches who stole cow's milk. This may well be the reason why 'hare' and 'rabbit' became taboo words and replaced by 'bunny'; while 'egg' was concealed as 'roundabout'. A sub-cultural language developed to deceive the clergy and thus avoid their inquisitorial wrath. Equally the egg games, over the centuries, became disguised as more acceptable ball games. Christina Hole (1979) suggested that some of the popular sports which evolved from the humble egg include football, bowls, handball, and ninepins (pp. 90-101).

But the significance of the egg pre-dates even Eastre and the celebration of Spring. The egg is to Pagan belief what the Garden of Eden is to Christianity — it accounts for the very origin of life. Rappoport (1930), in his *Superstitions of Sailors* book, cited a variety of universal folk myths which describe a Golden Egg from which the Universe sprang. In an extract from the Finnish-Russian *Kalevala* he quoted "On the third day... the eggs fell into the sea. From their lower portion came the Earth and from the upper portion the sublime Heaven. The white of the eggs constituted the Moon and the yolk the Sun" (pp. 17-19).

# Chapter 23

## FORBIDDEN COLOUR

QUOTE: *And so we fight them with our colours*
*nailed to the mast.* (Walter Scott)

Of all the colours of the rainbow, there is one which makes most Hessle Roaders twitch. It is a colour that affects everything from clothes to cars, from crews to pews, and even Christmas.

There is a Hessle Road saying which implies that "if a girl wears a dress of this colour, she'll not wear it out", and if a woman wears it she will "soon be wearing black" — widow's weeds. A bridesmaid's dress must never have a hint of it. And, according to Opie & Tatem (1989), in northern counties (1842) it must even be "excluded from the wedding dinner" (pp. 281-82).

There are various stories about coats of this colour being blamed for tragedy at sea. Frank 'Fat' Wilson, chief engineer with the Hellyer company for years, often cursed, "that bloody colour!". When his son Ron was killed aboard the *Kingston Pearl* (H.542) in February 1946 (Ch. 8) it was suddenly realised that one of his youngsters had a coat made of it. The coat was dyed black straight away. A Scottish lady who lives in Hull blamed a coat of this colour for the fact that she was made a war widow in February 1945. Her father-in-law had warned her "it will be followed by black" — and it was. Even Winston Churchill had an aversion to it. A local yarn goes that when he visited bomb-torn Boulevard off Hessle Road, he gave a man £10 to get rid of a jumper — it was green.

Annie Beadle scrimped and saved to buy some good-quality full-length curtains for Christmas 1929. Her big mistake was that these fashionable rainbow nets happened to contain a splash of green. It was only a bit, so she felt it did not matter. But her husband Walter was none too happy when he saw them go up in the bay window of their Woodcock Street terrace house. Her daughter Doreen Fleet recalls that "the next week when mam fell poorly, dad rove the nets down. Even though they were expensive he threw them in the dustbin".

Helen Crane always said, "I've had two good husbands" — but the cruel sea took them both. She first became a widow when Chris Pettman was washed overboard (along with several deckhands from a Hull trawler). She later married John Crane. He brought up the two Pettman girls as if they were his own. Together they had four more surviving children at No. 38 Manchester Street. After one particularly good trip John told Helen, "We'll see about Marsh Nicholson [furniture workshop] re-covering our old seven-piece suite" [couch, two armchairs and four chairs]. The colour they chose was a deep turquoise. Daughter Lily Thurston (83) recalls that "Mam went mad when the suite arrived back green". Helen complained to the shop, but they insisted that it was

99

the colour her husband ordered. So the Crane family were stuck with it. In July 1922 her husband John was cook aboard the Kingston's trawler *Agate* (H.338) in the North Sea fishing grounds. On a calm summer sea he disappeared. The last time he was seen alive was as he tipped a bucket of potato peelings over the side (HDM — 7 Jul. 22). "It was terrible when the pastor from the Fishermen's Bethel came and broke the news to our mum". In a deep state of grief Helen got rid of the cursed furniture.

Green paintwork also causes problems. Stan Cox tells the story of the loss of his first wife Rachel. As she lay on her death bed a very close friend rang to say, "I'm sorry Stan, but there is no way I'll cross that threshold because your front door is green". In October 1990 I got a phone call from the Hull City Council Architects Department. Whenever they painted any objects (doors, benches, lamp-posts) green they received complaints from the public, especially elderly people. They could not understand why this calming shade should cause offence, but realised "it was something to do with trawling".

Even Hull's car show-rooms are still affected. They refuse to stock a green motor vehicle because they are slow to sell. This same car-livery aversion was also displayed by land-speed record-breaker Donald Campbell. The *Daily Express* reported that he was rushed a Lotus sports car to test drive on the dangerous salt flats. "But he refused to go near it because of its colour" (15 Sep. 60). The owner of a large Gillett Street fish factory had a daughter killed by a green car. If any of his workers turned up in an overall of this colour he sent them home to change it, or sometimes bought them a new one.

The Hessle Road wool shop-keepers found a similar situation with their materials. This is a definite no-no colour when it comes to knitting baby clothes. Green woollen jumpers and mufflers (neck scarves) caused problems at sea. When Jim Fuller went from the cold deck up to the warm wheel-house he took off his muffler. The moment the skipper saw its colour he instantly grabbed it and hurled it out of the window into the raging sea. After Jim's protest, the Old Man agreed to buy him another one — but not the same colour — "That was out".

Eric Wedge, a trawlerman in the 1960s, never came across this colour taboo and even had a green suit which no one complained about at sea. But his experience seems the exception to prove the rule. Jenny Pattison from Easington, however, interviewed the Spurn life-boat men and they confirmed that there is still a strong superstition against green amongst east-coast fishermen and themselves. Proof that this taboo is here to stay comes from space travellers. Apparently, many NASA astronauts refuse both green and yellow in their space cabins (Haining, 1979, p. 29).

A Hessle Road Anglican vicar in 1924 decided to confront this colour taboo head on. Young Reverend Thomas Tardrew certainly caused a strong reaction. Even today, people love or hate him — there are no half-way feelings toward Tardrew. After many fundamental changes with the parish magazine and choir, he decided to have the beautiful redwood pews re-painted. He must have deliberately chosen the community's forbidden colour. It caused a dreadful outcry. Nevertheless, he obtained the desired effect and filled his Newington church for months afterwards. People came from far and near to St. John's. Neighbours had never seen so many cars parked in their streets.

*The controversial green pews of Reverend Tardrew can still be seen at St. John's Newington Church off Hessle Road. Thomas Tardrew had them painted in 1924. It seems he was not too popular with some families in the neighbourhood. When he held a garden party for the Archbishop of York the dignitaries were bombarded with stones, eggs, dead cats, and huge pieces of rotten cod – thrown by local youngsters. This recent picture (below) shows Reverend Derek Smith (and his wife Molly) during their retirement service on 21 February 1993.*
Copyright Alec Gill.

In December 1894 the Gallant family of West Dock Avenue adorned their home for the Christmas festivities. When their grandmother visited, the first thing she saw was the holly. She "blew her top" warning everyone that bad news was on its way. A few days later word came through that Wellington Gallant had been lost with the smack *John Sims* (H.1110) on 22 December in the North Sea. That same month fourteen other Hull trawlers were also lost. Even late into the 20th century, members of the Gallant family never display holly or any greenery indoors.

Lord Line bosun George Allan was very strict when it came to holly. Should a visitor bring any into his house, it was burned — he said it was unlucky to take it outside again. Greenery featured in other taboos at different times of the year. One day in May young Cordelia Brown excitedly brought home a twig of sweet-smelling blossom from Pickering Park. The moment her Gran saw it, Cordelia was angrily pushed into the back-yard, "Throw it out. You'll bring bad luck into the house!". Poor Cordelia learned yet another of her Gran's countless superstitions — the hard way. There is a Hampshire expression from 1923 which goes "If into the house you bring the May, / The head of the house will pass away" (Opie & Tatem, 1989, p.243). It is also claimed that May Blossom gives off a 'smell of death'. Cordelia also recalls being told to "never pick any dandelions or you'll pee the bed!" Two or three Hessle Roaders have mentioned, "Never burn anything green on the fire" — such as cabbage leaves — "they are things of life".

Set against these diverse stories about green there are many theories to explain why it is such an unlucky colour. One view is built upon the last few anecdotes about plants. Green is paramount in Nature — God's colour. Green-leafed trees in summer are followed by the black bark in winter. The summer-winter contrast of deciduous trees is green followed by black. Black symbolises mourning clothes. Therefore, to avoid death, avoid wearing green in the first place — yet another example of mimic magic. A further nature-centred view is that some seafarers describe the sea as being 'green'. And the trawlermen, for some reason, nickname cod fish 'Green' (Ch. 10).

A more light-hearted explanation comes from The Little People. There is an Irish sing-along game in which children ask what to wear at a funeral: "Shall we come in green?" But the counter verse is "Green is for the good people, You cannot come in that" — meaning the leprechauns. The national emblem of Ireland is the four-leafed clover, their favourite colour is green, and we often hear about the 'Luck of the Irish'. Green is lucky in the Emerald Isle, while for many Hull fishing families it is thought to be unlucky. But as Doreen Valiente (1975) pointed out, for those who have an affinity for green, it can be their lucky symbol (p.62).

From the mischievous elves, pixies and imps it is not too long before the researcher is confronted by The Green Man. Hull poet Audrey Dunne put me on this trail with the loan of Tolkien's (1975) *Sir Gawain and the Green Knight* — "All of green were they made, both garments and man" (p.18). An even more popular Green Man figure is Robin Hood. A green-clad hero pops up from time to time in various guises in both literature and folklore. He is also found in pubs and churches. There are drinking places called 'The Green Man', and a close look at some old-fashioned pub fronts show a man's face with vines and leaves. Better and striking examples can, however, be found at Beverley Minister. Verger George Dickinson said there are "a goodly number" of Green Men beneath the choir-stall seats. Each beautiful carving clearly shows a man's anguished look and greenery coming out of his mouth. All these church and pub artifacts are the physical forms of a forgotten ritual — while the colour taboo is its oral equivalent. The origin of the Green Man legend is weird and horrific — but logical within the culture from which it arose. Again we turn to the Celts for, what I now believe is, the true source of this taboo.

In his *Study of Magic and Religion*, Frazer (1922) has a section on 'The Burning of Men and Animals in the Fires'. Throughout Pagan Europe living people acted as symbols for the tree or corn-spirits. They "suffered death as such" during annual fire festivals. Furthermore, "condemned criminals were reserved by the Celts...at a great festival...once every five years...Colossal images of wicker-work or of wood and grass were constructed; these were filled with live men and animals; fire was then applied" (p.652-54). And so the prisoners in a wicker cage of leafy branches were sacrificed to the earth gods of vegetation. These sacrificial fire festivals created a vivid image in the minds of the ordinary village folk. It does not take much of a leap of the imagination to associate anyone clad in green with death. This is, I believe, the long-forgotten origin of the superstitions linked with green.

The topic of tabooed colours cannot be left without brief mention of red. Ginger-headed crewmen had a hard time with some skippers. It was common knowledge that skipper Walter Lewis of the *Lord Alexander* (H.12) would not go to sea with a red-haired man aboard. Arthur 'Ginger' Cowan decided, therefore, to wear a bowler hat to conceal his hair. It was only when the trawler was being clewed (cleaned) up for home that Arthur's bowler fell off in front of Lewis. Not being able to reconcile a bumper trip with an unlucky crewman, Walt sarcastically said, "How long have you been on board, then?". Opie & Tatem (1989) mentioned that in 1873 "red-haired children are supposed to indicate infidelity on the part of the mother" (p.325) — but gave no idea of the source of this superstition. It might simply be 'red for danger'.

Red and white flowers must never be placed together in a vase. Nor must they be taken to a hospital patient. They depict red blood on a white sheet — and thus death. On a more humorous note, these colours are perhaps disliked by Hessle Roaders because of their sporting affiliations. The local Hull F. C. rugby team colours are Black and White: their arch rivals across the river in East Hull — Kingston Rovers — wear Red and White.

A final red taboo states it is very unlucky for a ginger-headed person to 'first foot' on New Year's Day. This start-of-the-year taboo takes us into time magic.

George Allan (getting a wash on the boat deck) was a bosun with Lord Line for many years. He served longest aboard the **Lord Mountevans** (H.169). His daughter Joyce said he was highly superstitious, "he literally did the lot". One of George's strongest beliefs concerned green. He never allowed holly into his house. Yet Lord Line's trawler hulls were painted green. The contradiction is explained by a handicap which also prevented George getting his skipper's ticket – he was colour blind. Courtesy Joyce Allan.

*Lord Line Limited*

ENTIRE MANAGEMENT OF TRAWLERS UNDERTAKEN

TELEPHONES: 37697 (TWO LINES)
TELEGRAMS: ABOARD · HULL

YOUR REF WLC/G/AG.
OUR REF JHW/MP          ALL COMMUNICATIONS TO BE
                        ADDRESSED DIRECT TO THE COMPANY

ST. ANDREW'S DOCK

HULL

DIRECTORS: W. A. BENNETT, T. W. BOYD, D.S.O. (JOINT MANAGING), STEWART COLE, F.C.A., W. MALLOCH, B.SC. (ENG.) P. BENNETT, J. BENNETT, J. A. MALTON.

17th November, 1955.

## Chapter 24

## FRIDAY THE 13th.

PLAY: *He who laughs on Friday*
*will weep on Sunday.* (Racine)

PROVERB: *A Friday moon brings foul weather.*

Folklore has spun magic around time and numbers. The point at which both cross, superstitiously, is Friday the 13th. We will come to that in good time.

We begin at the beginning with New Year's Day. "First footing", recalled Ursula Wright (102), "always had to be by a dark-haired man. There was uproar if a woman was first to enter our house. It was unlucky for you and her". A male caller usually brought simple gifts like a piece of coal, wood, silver (6d. coin) and bread. Ursula added "these were kept religiously and then given back to him the next year". They are symbolic of life's basics: warmth, wealth and food.

Trawler bosun George Allan took 'seeing-in-the-New-Year' very, very seriously. Just before midnight he stood on his door-step with a shovel. Upon this was coal, firewood, a silver six-pence and slice of bread. Then he listened with ears pricked for the ships moored in the Hull docks. They started to blast away at their hooters on the stroke of midnight. He left the front door wide open to let in the New Year, and opened the back one to let out the Old. He then went around the house opening all the windows too. His wife Hilda and daughters Joyce and Norma always complained of the freezing cold. Apparently, the men who lived along Greenwood Avenue in North Hull used to line up outside their houses for the same New Year ritual — they chatted to each other as midnight approached.

There are lots of 'do not's' for New Year's Day. Betty Abel recalls that people "never shook a mat that day because that would shake a man overboard". Equally, "don't peg out clothes or someone will 'peg out' in the family". Another mimic magic restriction was never wash clothes on that day. To do so "washes one of the family away during the coming year".

The Pawson's were a Hessle Road family who suffered a loss which linked with this transgression. Maud Pawson had already lost her husband Richard, killed by gunfire from a German U-boat on 20 June 1918 aboard the Hull trawler *Aisne* (H.343). Fifteen years later, in January 1933, her 20-year old son Arthur was on the *Cape Delgado* (H.47) for a Christmas fishing trip to the White Sea under the command of Skipper Gillard. This Hudson ship was the second of five Hull losses that savage winter. The *Delgado* was last seen steaming home through the Norwegian fjords. She was "presumed lost with all hands" — sixteen crewmen. Arthur was spare-hand, loved the sea, always played tricks, and had an impulsive nature. He had been brought up mainly by his oldest sister Ivy because their mother was continually depressed after she became a war widow. Later, when Ivy married, Arthur always made a fuss of her young family. He took her son Wilfred Dawson to Hull Fair in the October before the fatal trip. When news came through of her beloved brother's loss, Ivy's thoughts immediately sprang back to New Year's Day. She had broken the strict time taboo and done her family washing that day. This superstition played guiltily on her mind — she "had washed her brother Arthur out of her family".

Anguish was heightened in that Arthur was to have been engaged upon his return. A special engagement cake had already arrived at his mother's home. On top was a tiny model of a trawler. No one in the Pawson family was allowed to eat that cake. It was kept for weeks and then months in the hope against hope that their Arthur would return out of the blue. Every January 15th, the anniversary of the loss, Maud remembered Arthur in the Memorial column of the *Hull Daily Mail* — "long after other families ceased to do so". And the model trawler — symbolic of the *Cape Delgado* — was kept under a bowl-shaped glass until Maud herself died in 1960. For her daughter Ivy this family tragedy only increased all her superstitious beliefs. So much so that she passed some of them onto her two daughters. Sixty years after the loss of their Uncle Arthur nieces Dorothy and Betty (who told me this sad story) never wash on New Year's Day.

Sunday is another special time when certain domestic jobs are taboo. No one was allowed to knit, touch scissors or even pick up a needle on the Sabbath. Leslie Copeman well remembers his widowed mother, "clipping me across the head because I got a needle out on a Sunday". Cutting nails and washing clothes were taboo in some families. Jean Gray, as well as not being allowed to sew a button, added that children were not allowed to play out on Sundays — especially not with a skipping rope. In pre-WWII years, Sunday School was the main activity and kids were dressed in their 'Sunday Best' — under strict orders "not to get messed up". In Robert Ramsbottom's family no one was allowed to wind wool after darkness fell — you would wind a man overboard.

More critical than the Christian Sunday was the Pagan Friday. Trawler-owner Terry Robins states that many of their West Dock Steam Fishing crewmen refused to sail on Fridays up until the 1950s. Landing on a Friday was even more disliked. But there is a strong practical motive behind this one. Fish-market prices were poor at the end of the week. Friday, the traditional fish-eating day, had obviously been missed. And fish kept over the weekend would not be too fresh by the time it got to the shops. But there may well be a more subtle superstitious reason why trawlermen avoided being on the fish dock on a Friday. That afternoon was jokingly called 'Fish Dock Races'. Pram-pushing women invaded St. Andrew's Dock to collect their men's basic weekly wage from the trawler-owners' offices. In other words, the trawlermen did not want to set sail knowing that women would be on the dock during that same day.

Before looking at the origin of this Friday taboo, it is worth inserting two verses kindly given by Cordelia Jones. One Saturday morning during the First World War, "I rushed down the stairs dying to tell mother about a nightmare — but mam refused to hear it". She subsequently told Cordelia the rhyme:

*Ivy Dawson (above) was very close to her younger brother Arthur Pawson. She had virtually brought him up since their widowed mother sank into a chronic depression with the loss of her husband aboard the **Aisne** (H.343) in the Great War. The Pawsons were a superstitious family and it was unlike Ivy to do her washing on New Year's Day 1933 – but she did (having a young family of her own). When news came through that Arthur was lost when the **Cape Delgado** (H.47) sank on 15 January, Ivy felt that she had washed her brother out of the family.*
Courtesy Betty Dawson & Dorothy Sharples.

*"Friday night's dream
On Saturday told
Is sure to come true
Be it ever so old."*

This is especially the case of a bad dream, and this is why her mother stopped her. Cordelia added another pithy rhyme: *"Friday flit, / Short sit"* (care is needed not to say this too quickly!). The belief is you will not stay too long at your new house if you move on a Friday.

Many people mention that Friday is unlucky because Jesus was crucified on that day. Apparently, there is a Yorkshire version of what happened to Christ as he carried the cross to Calvary. It is said He passed a woman who was washing clothes outside her house and she derisively waved a wet garment in his face. Christ is supposed to have cursed her and all those who wash on that day. Another view is that Friday is ill-fated because that is when Eve tempted Adam with the forbidden fruit (Waring, 1978, p.98).

I prefer a pre-Christian source to explain this time magic. Friday is the one day of the week which is named after a woman. She is the Nordic goddess Freya or Frigg (Guerber, 1908, p.135). Her chariot was sometimes drawn by a golden-bristled boar (Ch. 18), but more often by a team of cats — her favourite animal (an emblem of fecundity — Ch. 17). Frigg, Queen of the Gods, "possessed knowledge of the future" (p.42). She had a palace by the sea where she wove long webs of bright coloured clouds (p.43). The tall, beautiful Goddess had her special attendants who were magical maidens. Some legends link her with Valkyrie whose kiss of death transports the victim to Valhalla. In German myth Freya presides over the weather (p.51). Mariners from time immemorial, therefore, have strong cause to be wary of her and be careful not to set sail on the day dedicated to her. Guerber (1908) mentioned that "when Christianity was introduced into northern Europe...Freya herself, like all heathen divinities, was declared a demon or witch" (p.137). Besides being a swear word, Frigg survives everytime we mention the fifth day of the week (and five is the number of the Goddess). When this female Friday falls on the thirteenth day of the month, then there is increased danger for those who are superstitious.

Hull's St. Andrew's Fish Dock abounded with tales about Friday the 13th. Derek Coates was an instructor at the Nautical College (Boulevard) and taught trawlermen on radar courses. Certificates were duly awarded on the last Friday of their fortnight in class. If ever that day fell on the ominous date, there was pandemonium. "Every man refused to have his certificate dated Friday 13th because that was bad luck". Poor Derek was forced to mis-date the documents either the 12th or 14th.

Whenever a crew joined a new trawler there was always one member at least who paid attention to the H-registration number. Wilf Vines, writing in the *Fishing Years* (No. 4, May 90, p.17), described his pleasure trip as an eleven-year old aboard the *Lord Plender* in August 1934. He mentioned Arthur Carver who commented "about the ship having an unlucky number (H.517 = 13). I found out later that her number had been changed after war service" [H.191].

108

All these stories are from the past. But the No. 13 taboo is as vibrant today as it ever was. There are some Hull streets where numbers leap from 11 to 15 — like in Coronation Road South. The tall Hull Royal Infirmary is another brilliant example. The top floor — children's ward — should be No. 13, but it is not. The 12th floor accommodates Wards 12 and 120. But those above are 130 East and 130 West. Avoiding the use of the actual number does not mean, apparently, that bad luck will not strike. In March 1992 part of the roof collapsed. Fortunately, the ward area was empty and no one was injured. A Hospital Director was at a loss to explain why it happened. The *Hull Daily Mail* reporter, however, failed to get the Director's view on the fact that the incident occurred on Friday the 13th. As we saw with the green taboo, so No. 13 has found a place in futuristic space travel. NASA scientists were determined not just to conquer space, but also superstition. They decided to launch an Apollo 13 mission. It may just be coincidence, of course, but serious problems struck this moon flight on Monday the 13th April (Haining, 1979, p.29).

Whenever I ask an audience where 'unlucky 13' comes from, the frequent response is 'The Last Supper'. Prior to the crucifixion Jesus ate with his twelve disciples — thereby a link between 13 and his death has been formed. Indeed, it is considered a serious blunder if a host has thirteen guests at one table. This Last Supper view is interesting, but does not stand up to close examination. Whenever Christ did anything with all of his disciples, there were thirteen of them. We do not cite these earlier activities as being unlucky. Moreover, to seriously suggest that The Last Supper is unlucky is surely to undermine the whole basis upon which Christianity is built — the Crucifixion. Had Christ not died on the cross, Christianity would not have progressed — and is that an unlucky development? The same logic applies to Friday — after all, it is called 'Good Friday' by the Church.

The Pagan claim on No. 13 is stronger. Unlike our twelve calendar months, there are thirteen lunar months per year. Frigg was also Goddess of the Moon. The thirteen moon cycles control the turbulent seas of our planet. Every tide-time seafarers are reminded of the power of the moon which controls their fate. The mysterious moon also controls the female menstrual cycle (and is associated with lunacy). Ancient fishermen feared local witches who gathered together in a coven of thirteen women. So when this female number falls on the only feminine day of the week — Friday — there is "Double, double toil and trouble" (Macbeth, Act IV/i/10).

Moon magic too has a big influence upon superstitious thinking. Cordelia Jones recalls that, "Gran always drew the curtains if a new moon was out and told grandad to turn the money over in his pocket". Sometimes he dashed out into the back-yard with his little grand-daughter and he jingled the coins in his trousers pocket — to turn his money over — and only then could they look up at the new moon. The view in the community was "never look at the moon through a window pane". This echoes the older taboo of not looking at the moon through the branches of a tree. Perhaps there is a clash between the moon goddess and the tree spirits. And so this taboo transferred indoors (glass also has magical properties — Ch. 21).

In the Allan family, husband George could tell the level of the Hull tide by

*Frigg was the Scandinavian Goddess of Spring. She also had influence over the moon and tides – yet a further reason fishermen were in awe of her power. In Pagan Britain, some communities worshipped her. It is suggested that Fridaythorpe (Yorkshire Wolds), was once known as 'Frigg's Folk'. Guerber (1908) said that when Christianity took over female-worshipping villages, they named the church after a woman (p.137). It is, therefore, perhaps no accident that the 12th century Norman Church at Fridaythorpe is dedicated to the Virgin Mary.*

Copyright Alec Gill.

110

the position of the moon: "It's going to be a tea-time tide tomorrow". He was born on the 13th (Aug. 1901) and followed all the rituals to the Nth. degree. His daughter Joyce said, "he literally did the lot". He was well-versed in weather lore by observing the moon, winds, clouds and his beloved barometer. His wife Hilda would ask, "Shall I hang the washing out?" Even on a sunny morning he would look outdoors and say "No, don't bother, it'll be raining by dinner" —and it did. His daughter does not remember his weather omens, but I have since come across some superstitious tips: If the 'horns' of a new moon point slightly upwards, the next 28 days will be fine; but if down, it will be wet. Rain will follow if a full outline can be seen between the horns, or if there is a halo around any moon — "A ring around the moon / and rain comes soon". A new moon on a Saturday or Sunday results in rain and general ill-luck. And, finally, two full moons in the same month are a sign of bad weather — added to which, the second one is supposed to be a 'blue moon'.

I will end this section by returning to St. Andrew's Dock. It is a Thursday evening coming up to midnight in May 1938. The *Arctic Ranger* (H.429) is preparing to sail when Boyd Line ships' runner Alf Stockdale comes aboard to see Skipper Jack 'Hambone' Hamling (Jack got this culinary nickname because the trawler cook has to bring him soup with hambone in it at 3 a.m. every morning). Alf knows full well how superstitious Hambone is and so wryly asks, "You've picked a right day to sail, haven't you skipper?"

"What do yer mean?"

"Well, it's just turned Friday the 13th".

"That's it! We'll sail Monday", Jack declares as he leaves the *Ranger*. His crew get an unexpected weekend at home.

But whenever Hull trawlermen left the fish dock behind, they did not leave taboo-ridden objects behind. There were lots of things aboard to keep them on their superstitious toes.

# Chapter 25

## ARCTIC MAGIC

SAYING: *Worse things happen at sea.*

*OBJECTS AFLOAT*

In looking at magic items at sea what better place to start than with the ship *Herself*. No matter what name was given to the ship, it was usually referred to as 'She'. This applied even to a trawler with a name like *Thomas Hardy* (H.257). Perhaps the 'she' is seen as a nurturing mother figure who protects the men from the cruel sea.

The ship's bell is the embodiment of the trawler's soul. If it rings of its own accord then the vessel is doomed. There is a similar shore-based belief. If drinking glasses ring after being accidentally knocked, the tone must be stopped or else a sailor will be drowned. In Pagan temples the bell's outer shell was regarded as female and the clanger as male (Blackcat, 1988, p.194).

Ernie Suddaby mentioned that "some skippers went mad if they saw the fish-room hatch turned upside down". If the loose lid was turned over, according to mimic magic, so too the ship might turn turtle. Trawler cook Clarrie Wilcockson was always told, "Never leave a brush on the hatch — or you'll brush away your luck".

The next mystery revolves around the ship's mast and takes us back to nautical antiquity. Trawlerman Jim Fuller described a natural phenomena he observed on various trawlers "when stood on the bridge with now't to do. This Will o' the Wisp light jumped about in the rigging — never staying in the same place — from the main-mast to the wireless mast. Like a fire-fly it glinted in the night — but only small flashes of light. It is called St. Elmo's Fire". Radford (1974) described this as a "bright glowing light caused by electrical discharge during storms...Legend connects it with St. Elmo — the patron saint of seamen" (p.295). Apparently, he was dying at sea during a frantic storm. In his final breath he promised to return if the crew were destined to survive. After he passed away, strange lights flickered around the mast and the crew assumed it was the saint's message that they would live. This story is paralleled in the Greek legend of *Jason and the Argonauts*. Instead of St. Elmo, heroes Castor and Pollux are credited with the magical powers to protect sailors in distress. A more detailed account of this natural phenomenon is found in Rappoport (1930, pp. 47-61). It may be stretching the point, but is there 'correspondence' between St. Elmo's Fire at sea and lightning ashore in the community? We saw earlier how some families panicked in a thunder storm and frantically covered cutlery and mirrors (Ch. 21). This fire/lightning magic is important later (Ch. 32).

After surviving the storm, it is time for a well-deserved mug of tea — but even here there is a need to be careful. The English tea-drinking habit also

*Mariners the world over were amazed by St. Elmo's Fire. If the flashing balls
of light played around the top of the rigging it was a sign of fair weather,
but if it came lower down the mast there would be a storm. The Romans called this natural
phenomena Castor & Pollux; in other places it was Helen's Fire, or Corposant –
meaning 'holy body' (Brewer, 1990, p.271). In 1914, St. Andrew's Steam Fishing
launched the **St. Elmo** (H.3) at Beverley. She survived the war, but was wrecked on
the south coast of Iceland on 6 March 1921 – her crew were saved – as were
those legendary sailors who met St. Elmo himself (Ch. 25).*
Courtesy Malcolm Fussey/Christian Ford (Barnard print).

attracts taboos. A skipper on the Henriksen trawlers never emptied the tea-pot after fishing started — it was bad luck. More and more tea was added [as a weak-tea drinker, I find this habit foul!]. Likewise, in the Rilatt family, Laura never emptied or washed the tea-pot the day her Ted set sail. She always left it until the next day. At a talk to the Swanland Wine Guild, I was told of a family who, like the Henriksen skipper, never emptied their tea-pot until the man returned safe and sound — again, more tea was heaped into the pot! The underlying principle is probably inspired by mimic magic. The tea-pot might be seen as the trawler's fish room, with the leaves as symbolic fish filling up the trawler for a good trip. To empty the pot might either make the ship turn over or result in a poor catch.

A mug of tea must never be passed through the wheelhouse window or a porthole. It must be brought through the door. Bill Lewis knew of this belief and added, "it is a sign of a shipwreck". He guessed at a practical explanation: "the porthole might be the men's only means of escape, so it should not be blocked". The nearest analogy is that nothing should be passed through the rungs of a ladder. In ancient mythology, the 'ladder to heaven' must be respected. To reach through (or walk under) is a sinful act. So perhaps this thinking has been transferred to the soul-like properties of a ship at sea.

A tin of meat, milk or whatever must never be opened upside down. As the tea-pot, the tin may be analogous to the ship. This taboo fits in with what Terry Layden was told as a boy growing up on Hessle Road: "Never kick an empty tin [along the street] when your dad's at sea, because it is unlucky".

Pearls are seen as a bad omen — "pearls for tears". Equally, sea-shells are rarely found in the décor of a Hessle Road home. Both have come from the seabed. And if the sea gods realise that something precious has been taken from them, they will likewise take a loved one from you. In the literature, pearls are "a stone of the sea associated with the moon — owing to its influence over the tides" (Blackcat, 1988, p.212). The story of the *Kingston Pearl* (H.542) was unlucky for the Wilson family after she changed her name from the *Scottish* (Ch. 8). Les Harrington says that "old fishermen used to believe that if you wore a gold ring in one ear, you'd have good eye-sight". The joke is "How many sailors do you see with spectacles?". A practical explanation is that the gold paid for a decent burial should a mariner's body be washed up on some foreign shore.

Some trawlermen carried a protective talisman to sea. Little items were carried — endowed with protective properties — such as a bent penny, a lucky half-penny, a tiny sixpence from mother's Christmas pudding saved from boyhood, or a piece of cloth from the jacket pocket of a favourite, worn-out Lord Lovatt suit. But Brian Hawkins has a nice little story from when he first went trawling aboard *St. Alcuin* (H.125) in 1972. Aged about 17-years old, he was due to sail with his friend Pete — who backed out at the last minute. The night before Brian set sail, Pete said, "Here! Take this for luck — it'll protect you are sea". It was a small brass St. Christopher medallion. On the back was printed 'Hell's Angels', but his friend covered over the letters with a miniature dart-board. Brian always wore it for luck. Whenever he got his bunk sorted on a ship, he hung it at the head.

There is a general superstition "not to change any item of clothing put on inside out or you'll change your luck". The way in which this taboo was enacted aboard the *Joseph Conrad* (H.161) was filmed in a BBC television documentary called *"Fish Is The Living"* (1968). The skipper at that time was Dick 'Old Fox' Taylor. It showed that when the fish came aboard in good-sized bags, he never removed his cap, washed, shaved, or undressed. He feared that any change would change his luck and stop the fish being caught —mimic magic strikes again.


*TOUCH IRON*

In the taboo-ridden trawling world, it is difficult to avoid ominous words, sacred animals, forbidden actions and magic objects. It is easy to get caught out. Besides charms, there is a protective word to avert the dire consequences of a transgressed taboo. Everyone knows about 'touching wood'. But for fishermen, it is 'cold iron'. Hessle Road barber Tom Hollome was popular with trawlermen who had just landed and wanted to get smartened up. His son Les recalls that if a crewman overheard a forbidden word like 'pig', the fisherman repeatedly said, "Hot Iron, Cold Iron" until it was corrected (by that person correctly saying 'grunter'). If a tabooed utterance occurred at sea, some men reached for cold iron to avert the danger. Similarly, Scottish fishermen "would always cry out 'Cauld Iron!' and catch hold of the nearest piece of iron should anyone mention the name of the Deity" (Anson, 1932, p.85). There is an old school rhyme, *"Touch wood – no good; / Touch iron – rely on"*.

The best everyday example which testifies to a belief in the protective power of iron is the Lucky Horse-shoe. Eileen Wright told me, "it must never be hung upside down or you'll loose all the luck out of it". I have only come across one horse-shoe aboard a Hull trawler, but they were common on the wooden sailing smacks, and even Lord Nelson had one nailed to the mast of the *Victory* — though it let him down in the end. Just thinking about the correct way to position a horse-shoe, there is perhaps a subconscious reason why it has to be hung upwards. In its upright 'U' direction it is like a happy smile; the downward 'n' is more of a sad frown of someone who is unhappy (or unlucky). In some respects, the correct way it is hung is irrelevant. The thing which is lucky is not the horse-shoe itself, but the metal from which it is made — iron.

Iron has pride of place in the realm of metal magic. It provides universal protection against ghosts, the Devil, fairies, the Evil Eye, dragons, and lightning. The Egyptians and Aztecs called it "a gift from the gods". It is found in meteorites from the heavens. Warriors with iron weapons were superior to those with stone and bronze weapons. The cradle of civilisation was forged in iron. Whoever wielded an iron sword was a fighter with magical powers. With iron in hand, the Celtic tribes swept across Europe. The blacksmith who forged iron was a natural magician. For these old folklore reasons, the Hull trawlermen valued 'cold iron' to protect them in times of trouble.


## MONEY SCRAMBLE

Robert Ramsbottom declared that, "trawlermen spent money like crazy, so as not to take any back to sea". A similar view is "they earned money like horses but spent it like asses". A skipper went to see his wife in the old Cottingham Road Maternity Hospital. He was just about to leave when he turned around, reached into his pocket and, giving her a bundle of notes, said "There, you might as well have this". After he left, the mother explained to the women in the next bed, "He's very superstitious — never takes money to sea 'cos it'll mean a bad trip".

A popular image of a fisherman ashore is of him in a pub "splashing his money around buying drinks". Life-long trawlerman David Williams was often heard to say, "Money is made round and to go round". The wild character Dillinger "would never lend money — he'd rather give it to you. It was his superstition". Opie & Tatem (1989) mentioned that fishermen do not borrow from each others' boats or "the luck of the fishing goes with the article" (p.ix). This perhaps explains why Hull skippers preferred to pinch trawl gear from another ship in dock rather than ask to borrow it. "A fisherman's life was lived for the next trip", explains George Flitton, "If hard up, he'd say to his wife 'Never mind luv, we'll be alright next trip — it'll come out of the cod-end'".

One outcome of the above way of life was that a Hull trawlerman "was seen as being generous with his money". After good settlings, he had lots of money to spend during his short time ashore. So it went on booze, taxis, gifts, back-handers, gambling — especially the young deckie-learners. If they failed to spend it before returning to sea, some gave or threw it away. One man always left money behind the bar in Rayner's "for his mates to have a final drink on him if he failed to return". Others gave it to children — if not their own, any in the street they happened to meet. Chief engineer James Cullen — who went trawling from eleven-years old — used to hide his left-over coins downstairs in his Somerset Street house for his kids to find in the morning. Vera Turnbull recalls how "dad used to reach into his pocket for all his loose change, and say to the kids 'Who wants to play scrambles?' and throw fistfuls of money for everyone to get. I had lots of friends when dad was home".

Eric Wedge has happy boyhood memories of him and his pals going up to trawlermen to ask "Are you gonna do a scramble Mister?" The best one down his street (Strickland) was Jim Patterson (c.1953). Lads regularly went 'scrambling' outside pubs — "it was just another way to get cash, 'cos we didn't get any pocket money".

There is a tragic tale associated with the giving of money away before departure. This anecdote also demonstrates a subtle clash between two superstitions. In January 1968, Susan Peach was home at Fern Grove (Division Road) when her uncle arrived unexpectedly. Harry Riches — nicknamed 'Cockney' because he came from London — was on his way to catch a plane to Reykjavik. He had to replace the cook of the *Kingston Peridot* (H.223) who had fallen ill and had been landed at Iceland. Sue recalls her Uncle Harry coming in and placing all his loose change on the ktchen table, along with a little pair of dark brown scissors. Sue's superstitious mother, Maureen, was unhappy to accept the scissors without giving Harry a payment in exchange. She obviously subscribed to the view expressed by Waring (1978) that, "many folk maintain it is bad luck to accept a present of a pair of scissors without giving a small coin in return to the donor" (p.201). The belief in Hull is that if the scissors (or any sharp item) are accepted without any payment, then the person who takes the pair 'cuts the friendship'. Equally, the problem for 'Cockney' was that he could not take any money off to sea with him — that was why he had popped around to leave his loose change and to say where he was going. Therefore, he refused the token payment. It was left at that because he was in a rush to get on his way.

When the terrible news came through that the *Kingston Peridot* had been 'lost with all hands' on the 26 January 1968 off northern Iceland, Maureen felt she had 'cut' the link with a member of her family. Incidentally, there was another broken taboo related to the loss of the *Peridot*. There were not only two brothers aboard — Peter (mate) and Robert (sparehand) — but their surname had an 'S' in it: Smith. This brother aspect parallels the tragedy of the Williams family with incidents aboard the *Boston Lincoln* and *St. Benedict* (Ch. 8 & 16).

When Hull trawlers left the St. Andrew's Dock lockpit at the start of a new trip, some men threw any loose change into the Humber. Alf Louth recalls this happening during his five years at sea (1958-63): "fist-fuls of money were slung over the side. The feeling was that if you went away skint, you'd land a good

116

trip" (7/93). There is, however, a strong superstitious motive hidden beneath this 'throwing and giving money away' behaviour. If trawlermen returned to sea with pockets full of money, the sea gods will realise they are rich and so give them a poor trip. The *Reader's Digest* (1977) mentioned that fishermen "spit on a coin and throw it overboard" (p.ix). Arthur Beal tells the story of a Hull skipper "having a run of poor hauls. In despair he reached into his pocket for all his loose change and hurled it into the sea saying 'If I can't catch it, I'll buy the f...ing fish".

We have come full circle. From beginning with sailing-day taboos (Part One), we have ended with the men back at sea for another trip — with no escape from the endless fishing superstitions. We have looked at the women ashore, the men afloat, animal taboos and object magic. These stories are just the tip of the iceberg. We now need to go below the surface to see what lurks beneath this weight of superstitious beliefs in the magical Hessle Road community.

# PART FIVE
## 'FEAR OF THE GODS'

### Chapter 26
### ROOT MEANINGS

PROVERB: *The gods do not deduct*
*from our allotted span the hours*
*spent in fishing.* (Babylonian)

We have trawled through a sea of superstition. The catch is stacked from Parts One to Four. We now need to make something of it all. Why was there such a high level of 'Superstition and Folk Magic in Hull's Fishing Community'? One way to begin answering this question is to examine the meanings of the key words used throughout this book.


*SUPERSTITION*

As a historian, I love to get down to the root meaning of words. But with a word like 'superstition' it is not easy because it has been re-defined so many times over the centuries, and not always from the best of motives. An added distortion is that superstitious rituals have long been ridiculed as illogical by academics (and others in authority) and so ignored as a serious topic of research. Nevertheless, it is vital to establish the primary meaning of this word for the present work. Only in their original context, I believe, can the Hessle Road superstitions make sense. The word's modern, blinkered usage, only encourages a trivial attitude toward what is, after all, the basic level of emotional thinking of our ancestors, and the one to which we fall back upon when confronted by a life-or-death situation.

In my quest for the initial source meaning, I was greatly helped by an article in the *Encyclopædia of Religion* called 'Superstition'. Mary O'Neil (1987) traced its classical usage to *'deisidaimonia'* — a Greek word which described a *'cringing, obsessive fear of the gods'*. This root definition gives much more stress upon the emotional element in superstitious behaviour — an aspect I wish to expand throughout the whole of Part Five. I will adapt a modified version of this classical meaning as we proceed. In the meantime, it is important to outline a brief history of what has happened to this word since its early Greek days as it has been re-cycled many times over up to the present day.

A major re-definition came with the Latin word *'superstitio'* (from which we get our English word, of course). This new Roman perspective gave partial insight into the word, but added much more confusion to its meaning. A direct translation of *'superstitio'* is 'surviving, witnessing'. O'Neil stated that it "included the idea of *surviving* an event [such as a battle or storm] as a *witness* and referred originally to divination concerning the past, the power to witness a distant event as though it were present" (p.163 my italics) — as would a gripping story-teller in the oral tradition.

It is only a thin line between 'witnessing' *past* and *future* events. And so the same '*superstitio*' label was easily attached to divination (interpreting, say, the behaviour of birds — '*winged messengers of the gods*' — as a sign of someone's pending death — Ch. 16). This simple metaphysical move — going beyond the physical event — was soon classed as magic, and condemned by the more logically-minded in Rome. Thus the Latin word rapidly acquired a derogatory meaning.

Indeed, the renowned Roman philosopher Cicero gave a darker definition to the word and set a standard for centuries to follow. O'Neil summed up the Cicero view as "*superstitio* meant erroneous, false or excessive religious behaviours stemming from ignorance of philosophical and scientific truths about the laws of nature... associated with the common people (*vulgus*) and with the countryside (*pagus*)...a social locus in the uneducated, lower orders of Roman society" (p.163).

Then something subtle, but profound happened to the word: it was gradually used in a dismissive manner to describe "any exotic foreign religions of which the Romans disapproved" (p.163). And the false idea gradually came about that any superstitious behaviour was something which had merely 'survived' from the past — a relic of bygone days. It is plain to see that the classical Greek meaning was soon buried. The emotional element — '*fear of the gods*' — was replaced by a more politically-loaded definition — used to attack the religious faith of foreigners and reject any beliefs which did not comply with their own. I wish to revitalise the original Greek definition — thus I have called Part Five '*Fear of the Gods*'.

This pluralistic reference to 'gods', instead of singular God, indicates that we are not dealing with the Jewish, Christian, or Islamic faith. The obvious view is that superstitious belief is rooted in Paganism. Cicero himself used the word '*pagus*' when he referred to the people of the countryside. So what does the word Pagan mean? Originally, to be a pagan was simply a rural peasant —an uneducated person, a labourer in the fields. As workers on the land they endured the vagaries of Nature. Similarly, trawlermen 'harvest the seas', are close to Nature, labour at the fishing grounds, and are at the mercy of the violent elements. This parallel in occupations is perhaps why the fishing families perpetuated many of the beliefs cherished by our pagan ancestors. The common denominator being their fearful dealings with the almighty forces of Nature.

Briefly then, I prefer to understand 'superstition' as meaning '*fear of the gods*' and Pagan is '*rural/working people*'. But what must be remembered is that these terms did not naturally arise from the people themselves. There were labels imposed upon them by writers from a higher social order who rarely came into direct contact with the ordinary folk in the fields (or at the fishing grounds).

Just as Greek power was replaced by Roman; so the Romans were deposed by Christianity. As the early Christians struggled to get a grip on Europe, they cleverly turned the word 'superstition', like a weapon, upon the Romans themselves. The new Church declared that "religion is the worship of the true, superstition is that of the false" (O'Neil, 1987, p.164). Extra force was neatly added by branding all previous gods and goddesses as demonic, and all pagan (folk) rituals and sacrifices as offerings to the Devil.

119

By 600 AD the peasants, however, had still not abandoned their popular magic, divination and worship of trees. Pope Gregory the First proposed that "heathen shrines be reconstructed as churches and... celebrations be adapted to the Christian calendar" (p.164). The winter solstice became Christmas, and the Midsummer Fire Festival became the Feast of St. John the Baptist. Softly-softly failed. The horrors of the Mediæval Inquisitions followed. The witch hunts and sorcery trials were instigated — mainly against the ordinary folk with women bearing the brunt of the venom. Yet centuries of blood-curdling torture and death also failed to exorcise superstitious belief from the hearts of the labouring families in villages and fishing ports around Europe.

The Church, indeed, cracked first with the mighty schism between Catholic and Protestant (1517 AD). The irony of ironies is that Papist religion was next branded with the stigma of superstition. The 'judge' was found guilty of crimes for which he had condemned others to be burned at the stake. This overlapping of one religion followed by another is summed up by Matthews (1988): "The gods of one people became the devils or faery-kind of the next one... A name which once inspired awe and reverence became an object of fear or mockery" (p.12). Over the centuries, therefore, the word 'superstition' was used as a political axe to swing at one's enemies.

Although the witch trials have now gone, 20th century ideas about superstition are still condemning. Thurston (1933) wrote, "superstition is a serious evil" (p.7) and "so far we have only dealt with those purely pagan superstitions which the Christian clergy, much to their credit, seem resolutely to have discountenanced and tried to suppress. The situation, however, was an extremely difficult one. The rude, uneducated populations with whom they had to deal were so wedded to the time-honoured festitivies...that it was impossible to break them of the habits" (p.69). In August 1984 a similar view was expressed by Father Michael Walter of the Newington parish (Hessle Road). He commented that "the English working-class church never got to the heart of the people. The Church filled a role in the past which television fills today — it was a pastime". He saw the Hessle Roaders as 'industrial peasants' and 'urban pagans'.

This view was again echoed in 1986 when the *Hull Daily Mail* ran the headline: "Pagan Hull's Poor Record Upsets Clergy". Reverend Peter Harrison of the Drypool parish (East Hull) was worried that "the number of church-goers has hit rock bottom. One of the causes could be connected with Hull's fishing industry and its superstitions" (27 Aug.). East Hull, incidentally, is sometimes referred to as "The Christian side of the River [Hull]" — perhaps because of the many chapels along Holderness Road. A Diocese of York leaflet came through our door recently (for a course in Sep. 1993) which declared that "the business of theology is to save religious faith from superstition, irrationality and plain nonsense" (p.2).

In addition to antagonism, there is sometimes misunderstanding about the source of specific superstitions. Within a Christian culture it is perhaps inevitable that people perceive long-held beliefs in a biblical light. A few examples of common mistakes are (with the older pagan origins in brackets) as follows: touching wood is said to acquire the protection of the Cross (tree spirits); No. 13

*I have argued the case that many Pagan superstitions have been given a false Christian veneer.
When on holiday in Brittany (1992) I came across this enormous Celtic standing stone which had
also been Christianised. This 40-foot high menhir provides a physical equivalent of what has
taken place over the centuries with various folk superstitions and beliefs. This picture was taken
near Pleumeur-Bodou, north of Lannion.*
Copyright Alec Gill.

is avoided because that number sat at The Last Supper (thirteen lunar months); Friday is unlucky because of Good Friday (female day named after Norse goddess Frigg); the Easter Egg depicts Christ's re-birth (Eastre is a Spring Goddess); and the Bible itself has been used in a superstitious manner, "a Christian, for example, may believe that in a time of trouble he will be guided by the Bible if he opens it at random and reads the text that first strikes his eye" (New Encyclopædia Britannica, 1979). This article concluded that "superstition has been deeply influential in world history. Being irrational, it should recede before education and, especially, science" (p. 684).

Science, indeed, is a new kind of 'god' and sits on the throne of power once occupied by religion. Like the latter, science too feels threatened, and vents its anger against fundamental superstitious thought. Nowadays it is trendy to rationalise superstition in the hope that it will wither away. Modern sceptics claim, "I don't walk under a ladder in case a pot of paint falls on my head". It sounds as if it already has. Some 'protest too much' that they are not superstitious — they deliberately go out of their way to spill salt and break mirrors (like The No. 13 Society) — so much so that it becomes an inverse superstition in itself. In a post-modernistic age, it is easy to overlook the true purpose of our ancient superstitions, and to blindly shun them all as nonsense.

But would nonsense continue over thousands of years if it contained no sense? Go into any Primary School and you will be amazed that the youngsters have scores of superstitions and add new ones all the time. Peter Haining (1979) cited the view of Eric Maple who made the refreshing point: "There are apparently no absolutely new superstitions but only ancient ones which, as if possessed by some diabolical instinct for survival, persist in advancing from generation to generation disguised as novelties" (p.21).

It is time to stop this condemnation. Science should learn from the failure of religion. Superstition is illogical. But the fact that it survives and thrives, provides great insight into the working of the human mind. This neglected and abused area demands both respect and research in the future — not dictatorial dismissal.

In summary, although the word 'superstition' is still used today as a derogatory term to condemn others who do not hold similar religious beliefs to one's own, I prefer to embrace the classical definition which describes the behaviour more as a psychological process. In conclusion, I wish to modify the original Greek idea and drop their 'cringing, obsessive' bit and focus upon the '*fear of the gods*' aspect. Furthermore, the word 'fear' does not necessarily have to always mean 'a painful emotion aroused by a sense of impending danger: alarm; dread' — but can be taken as 'awe' which is a mixture of both 'fear and admiration' (Collins). In other words, superstitious belief can also arise out of people being in '*awe of the gods*'.


## TABOO

This word also has a notorious and misunderstood past. Today, it is mainly taken to mean 'forbidden' or 'prohibited'. This impression has no doubt been reinforced by this book with stories of trawlermen forbidden to say 'pig' or wear green. But if we examine its root, we immediately see taboo behaviour in a more positive light. The word is non-European and has been corrupted by Western usage. It is from the Polynesian word '*tapu*' meaning 'consecrated' and describes "a system among the natives of the Pacific Islands by which certain objects and persons are set aside as *sacred*" (Collins — my italics). We can, therefore, look afresh at the people, actions, animals, and objects in the Hessle Road superstitions and see them as having a 'sacred' dimension. And by doing so, much of the nonsense aspect can be stripped away.

Sigmund Freud (1913) made an extensive study of this topic in his book *Totem and Taboo*. His definition can be applied to the Hessle Road culture. He stated that taboo has two contrary meanings: (a) sacred, consecreted; and (b) dangerous, forbidden, unclean. He looked at taboo behaviour in its wider context and made a number of points previously overlooked in this area. The taboo prohibitions are of unknown origin and are "the oldest human unwritten code of law...taboo is older than gods and dates back to a period before any kind of religion existed" (pp.18-19). With the earliest concept of law came the idea of punishment and "the violated taboo itself took vengeance. When, at a later stage, ideas of gods and spirits arose...the penalty was expected to follow automatically from the divine power...The violation of taboo makes the offender himself taboo".

This partly explains why some people were ostracised within the community (an unchurched mother or evil-eyed woman — Part One). Then Freud introduced an interesting notion which accounts for many trawling superstitions. There are "temporary taboos which may be attached to certain particular states, such as menstruation and child-birth, the warriors...or special activities such as fishing and hunting" (pp.20-21). 'Sailing day', therefore, can be seen as a 'particular state' which generates 'temporary taboos' (not washing, etc. — Ch. 1). Freud also highlighted the blind acceptance of the beliefs: "Every sort of thing is forbidden; but they have no idea why, and it does not occur to them to raise the question. On the contrary, they submit to the prohibitions... and feel convinced that any violation will be met by the direst punishment" (p.21) — a further reason for the '*fear of the gods*' definition.

Roy Wagner (1987) examined the mystical area of taboo within a social context. He claimed that '*tapu*' "relates the cosmic to human actions...controlling individual and social life...[by] segregating persons, objects, or activities that are divine or sacred, or those that are corrupt or polluting, from the common everyday realm". He cited fishing expeditions as an example where community-wide restrictions were imposed upon common activities (p.233). An everyday Hessle Road example would be the sailing-day taboos when women did not empty ash trays and fire grates, and dared not go on the fish dock (Ch. 1). And '*egg*', for example, is a taboo word that has significance far beyond its domestic usage. In its '*tapu*' sense it is 'sacred' — a symbol of fertility (Ch. 22).

Wagner highlighted a related Polynesian concept when describing the degrees of talent possessed by different workers in a community — "all have their *manu* which is capable of being lost or dispersed until the proper *tapu* is observed" (p.233). A trawling example of '*manu*' is a skipper's '*luck*' in catching fish. Finally, Wagner pointed out the danger of literal (direct) thinking when we look at any tabooed object, such as "pork is a potential carrier of trichinosis", therefore, avoid pig. His key point is that "taboo is usually indirect" (p.235). The reason a pig is referred to indirectly as 'grunter', therefore, is because it was a sacred (totem) creature in ancient times — and this belief has been kept alive within the Hessle Road culture through superstition. The taboos which surround 'curly-tail' are to protect ordinary folk from coming into direct contact with this holy animal. In trying to make sense of many superstitions it is vital to see taboo not (directly) as forbidden, but (indirectly) as objects and activities which were once holy and sacred to our ancestors in ancient times.

### OMEN

There is less confusion about this word. Omens are "the signs and warnings about the future — a frequent component of superstition" (Simons, 1973, p.4). Omens can be good or bad. A good omen is being born with a caul, a bad one is seeing a rat leave a trawler. A special feature of an omen is that it must be a message we did not seek — it comes along accidentally (indirectly), like an overheard word or a flying bird. Signs are all around, but we are not always alert and they are easily missed. Most omens are ominous and produce forebodings about the future (Ch. 31).

Throughout our search for the root meanings of the words 'superstition', 'taboo', and 'omen' we have kept bumping into the idea of certain beliefs being 'indirect'. This hidden component is crucial in our attempt to make sense of what some see as nonsense. Another word to partially explain what I mean by 'indirect' is 'subconscious'. Superstitious actions are rarely addressed to the conscious logical mind, but are subtle suggestions aimed at our deep-seated emotions. Superstitions are for the benefit of our inner psychology (Ch. 28).

*Superstitious practices are difficult to photograph. The animal magic rarely shows in physical form. A visit to Beverley Minster, however, provides many tangible examples of past beliefs. Above shows a Medieval knight in mortal combat with the dreaded wild boar (Ch. 18). Below is a Green Man with branches coming from his mouth – a figure sacrificed in druidic rituals (Ch. 23). These beautiful wooden carvings are hidden away; but can be found by lifting the choir-stall seats. Other Green Men can be spotted carved in stone elsewhere within the Minster. Search them out when you visit Beverley.*
Copyright Alec Gill.

## Chapter 27

## FOLK MAGIC

QUOTE: *It is the customary fate*
*of new truths to begin as heresies*
*and end up as superstitions.* (Thomas Huxley)

Superstition is rooted in folklore. The word 'folk' is used in the sense of 'ordinary, everyday people' — non-scholars — largely working-class people who struggle to do the best for themselves and their families. The word 'magic' is much more difficult to define.

Even in antiquity the word was highly debatable and used with disparaging overtones. Generally, the term is too broad for our needs. Betz (1987) stated that "the uses of magic seem to have been unlimited...ritual, myth, symbol, and even language in general [meaning: words have power]. Magic was presupposed in all forms of the miraculous, and in medicine, alchemy, astrology and divination" (p.93). For our purpose we can narrow magic down to the definition given by Frazer (1922, pp.11-48). He argued that sympathetic magic still persists in modern society as a substratum of superstition. Sympathetic magic takes three forms: (1) Imitative [or Mimic] Magic — the underlying principle is quite simple: 'like makes like' or 'an effect echoes its cause' (a *whistling* woman *whistling* up a storm at sea); (2) Contact [or Touch] Magic — again, the rule is fairly naïve: any two things which have been in direct physical contact still influence each other, even though they are far apart in time or space (an example is when a Hessle Road widow took her lost-at-sea husband's tie or cap to a Spiritualist meeting to find if he was really dead or alive); and (3) Mimic and Touch Magic can be combined: 'not washing on sailing day' is a powerful illustration of this double magic. By immersing her husband's jumper in a sink of water, not only does this physically mimic the washing of a trawlerman overboard and him being plunged beneath the water (waves), but also involves the submerging of an item of clothing which contained the essence of her husband because he had been in touch with it when worn. Perhaps the reason why the non-washing restriction caused such anxiety in the fishing community was because it was a combination of both Mimic and Touch magic.

Frazer added a further positive and negative dimension to his definition of magic. He saw the carrying of a charm as a positive precept — to attract good luck. Whereas the negative side is the taboos — by not doing something in order to avoid bad luck. Indeed, superstition is a two-edged sword of trying to attract good luck and avert bad luck with one thrust.

At the crux of all superstition and taboo is a causal link. For example, it is unlucky to look back. Therefore, looking back and bad luck are linked. The two are so strongly associated that one is mistakenly seen to cause the other.

126

There is a perceived cause-and-effect relationship. But correlation does not necessarily mean causation. Science experiments with correlation by the application of logic. Folklore wonders about correspondence through the mystery of magic.

Magic is a means of managing the mysterious cause-and-effect links in life. Associations are made in the mind and form correspondences between earthly events and the gods above who control our destiny. The occult outlook sees magic in everything: numbers, trees, mirrors, fires, days, food, colours, cauls, cutlery, animals, words, etc.. Following this line of thinking, I have drawn up a Table of Correspondences with Hessle Road links:

| SUPERSTITIOUS CATEGORY | SACRED TO HESSLE ROAD |
|---|---|
| ANIMAL | PIG / FISH / BIRD |
| NUMBER | 13 |
| TREE | HAZEL |
| JEWEL | PEARL |
| COLOUR | GREEN |
| PLANET | MOON |
| METAL | IRON |
| WORD | NICKNAME |
| DAY | FRIDAY |
| ELEMENT | FIRE / WATER |

We are, of course, dealing with the psychological association of ideas upon which our ancestors' primitive thinking was based. Magical notions were born when *homeo sapiens* looked at Nature through wondrous eyes. These earliest human memories and mental habits linger in the human psyche. When superstitions burst to the surface they provide a privileged peep into our primitive past. And they retain an important, largely unexamined, role in the realm of human adaptation, creativity, emotionality, and psychology.

## Chapter 28

## PSYCHOLOGY

INAUGURAL ADDRESS: *The only thing we have to fear
is fear itself.* (Franklin Roosevelt)

Many areas of psychology inter-twine with superstition. Indeed, our classical definition of the word superstition — '*excessive fear of the gods*' — is one entirely based upon emotion. This line of argument is supported by Jahoda (1969). He pointed out that, "in spite of the sharp divergence between the positions of Freud and Jung...both agree that superstitious beliefs and practices are deeply rooted in man's unconscious mental processes, both held that superstition is not a thing of the past, or confined to the less educated — it is regarded as part of everybody's mental make-up and liable to come to the surface under certain circumstances...Above all, they stress the emotional element in superstition, which helps us to understand why confronting the superstitious person with contradictory information often makes so little difference" (p.69). From this psychoanalytic approach we go to the other extreme in the world of psychology — the Behaviourist.


### CONDITIONED BY NATURE

Human conditioning has been experimentally studied by the Behaviourists. Behaviourism is a narrow School of Psychology which reduces all behaviour to simple stimulus-and-response actions. Let us take the superstitious example of spilling salt. The spilt salt stimulates a throwing (over the left shoulder) response. This example is similar to Pavlov's classical experiment whereby the sound of a bell is conditioned in a dog's brain with food and produces a salivating response. In effect, any two previously unrelated events can be associated through conditioning. In superstitious terms, green is associated with death, and so a mental (not real) link is made between green and death.

The more complex taboos are best explained by Skinner's operant conditioning. If a skipper, for example, keeps his cap on while the fishing is good, he is less likely to remove it on the next trip when the fish start coming aboard. In psychological terms, if a behaviour is reinforced (rewarded by fish), this increases the chances of that 'operational' behaviour being repeated in the future. On the other hand, if a behaviour is punished (sailing on Friday the 13th followed by the loss of life at sea), then this increases the chances of that behaviour being avoided in the future. Thus, we learn through simple associations. Instead of the psychological jargon of reward and punishment, the Hessle Roaders simply attach the concepts of good luck and bad luck to specific situations, animals or objects.

Social reinforcement also plays a part, especially within such a close-knit community. There was pressure to conform to established superstitious rituals

*Superstitions are universal. This Chinese wooden-carved coffee-table top, purchased by George West in Singapore, illustrates the point. The oriental fishermen are lamenting the loss of their friend taken by the waves. They look down into the water, little knowing that he, or his soul, is overhead –being taken to heaven by a sacred bird. Hull trawlermen too associated birds with the souls of the dead (Ch. 16).*

Courtesy Valerie & George West.

(unchurched mothers turned away). Unwittingly, superstition has a built-in bias through selective reinforcement. Many trawlers did, over the years, sail on Friday the 13th without any tragic result. Yet it only takes one loss for someone to recall its ominous sailing date. We tend to confirm our pre-held views. Without going into the mechanics of Behaviourism, it is extremely difficult for superstitious thinking to fade out (extinguish) because it is on a variable-interval schedule of reinforcement. That is, no one knows when, how or why a taboo will be fulfilled (reinforced). In the absence of a tragedy, it is tedious if someone retrospectively dredges up ominous pre-events which were not fulfilled. So in this sense, superstition cannot lose the toss: 'Heads I win, Tails you lose'. Irrational, but essential.

## YIN-YANG

For some psychological reason, we like to keep irrational magic alive. This intuitive side is vital to the human psyche. In conversation with *I Ching* teacher

129

Sally Haden she stated, "we live too much in the rational world where everything is scientifically ordered and logical" (Yang). The danger is that a totally clinical outlook can cause an imbalance in the human personality. Balance comes from the irrational creative (Yin) side of our brain which sparks off abstract emotional associations and imaginative thoughts. This ancient Chinese *Taoist* philosophy has been studied by psychologists under the heading of 'brain hemisphere dominance'. Broadly speaking, our left hemisphere deals with the logical/rational world, while the right copes with the emotional/magical processes. Superstition is one route into our irrational mind which provides the mystery and magic to help us handle highly emotional situations.

## EMOTIONAL HIGH

The emotional side of life in Hull's fishing community (grief, guilt, luck, joy) has been expressed in various interviews. But Audrey Grady touched on many of the exhilarating feelings. A few snippets from her nine-page interview are: "Fishing is a game of chance; some skippers are lucky because they hit the good grounds, get fair weather, land for the right market...the Hessle Road shops benefited from the men's generous nature...in the winter it was dreadful... Everything was 'out of proportion' with three long weeks at sea and only two days at home to make up for their absence — it was overdone, too intense, an untrue life. It appeared glamorous when home with pockets full of money, taxi rides, pick up a girl, give back-handers. There was a feeling of power — but it was all disproportionate" (8/84).

This illustrates a life-style of *heightened emotions*. Their high-risk occupation forced men to *live life to the full*. One instance of how things were *over the top* is shown in the trawlerlads' flamboyant made-to-measure light-coloured suits with 28-inch bell-bottoms, another example was their overwhelming generosity (Ch. 25). Geoff Levy, owner of the Hessle Road Clothing House, said "there was no tomorrow because they did not know if they would return. They went a little berserk. They had to spend that money while ashore" (8/84). This living near the edge meant that their senses were much more heightened than shore-based factory workers in routine, repetitive jobs. This may account for why they and their families were more alert to the omens and premonitions (Ch. 31). And more suggestible to superstition than most.

## CONFRONTING REALITY

Based on the above it might be easy to get the wrong impression that the Hessle Roaders were escapists who did not live in the real world. But this view can be stood on its head. It was *because* they were very much in the dangerous harsh reality of working in the Arctic waters that they were subconsciously drawn into looking at the world through superstitious eyes. Given this 'protection' they could face whatever violent Nature threw at them. Folk magic was a shield between them and their daily danger. A fish dock joke was that many of the old trawlers were "floating rust boxes. A sober man would not take one into the Humber (or 'Picky Park' boating-lake), let alone the White Sea. You had to be drunk to go out in them". (It is only partly true about the ships. Hull has always been a pioneering port with the most up-to-date trawlers. Equally, the owners got the fullest life out of them and so some were past it.) Drunkenness was a serious aspect, however, especially for the young trawlerlads. Booze provided an initial cushion from the perilous side of their job, while the superstitions were a more long-term durable buffer. When surrounded by danger it is best not to focus directly upon it otherwise nerves can easily crack. The tight-rope walker does not look down. Again, we can see the value of dealing with the world in an 'indirect' manner (Ch. 26).

"Magical thinking", claimed German psychologist Wilhelm Wundt, "was based on emotional processes, the principal one being the fear of nature, which appears hostile to human well-being and which is conceptualised as an evil force that can be controlled by magic" (Middleton, 1987, p.84). Superstition is strongest where Nature is powerful. Jahoda (1969) put it more formally when he claimed "where chance and circumstance are not fully controlled by knowledge, man is more likely to resort to magic" (p.128). Fear, therefore, is transformed to optimism by simple folk magic in the guise of superstition. For example, by placing one's faith in a lucky charm, one can confidently brave the elements during the hunt for fish.

## Chapter 29

### 'LAST OF THE HUNTERS'

POEM: *Home is the sailor, home from the sea,*
*And the hunter, home from the hill.*
(Robert L. Stevenson)

A lot of fishing superstition arises from the fact that trawlermen are predators: *'The Last of the Hunters'* — their living comes from killing.

Primitive hunters credited animals with immortal souls. Great respect was paid to the fish. The dual purpose being to protect the fishermen's soul from the vengeful spirits of the dead fish, and to ensure future abundance (Frazer, 1922, pp.518-29). Ancient fishermen were careful "to propitiate the spirits of the animals" (Ibid, p.127) — to gain favour of, appease, and conciliate the souls of their countless victims. Hunt magic absolved primitive fishermen of their guilt. Hull's industrial trawlermen, however, lacked an equivalent social ritual to ease their subconscious guilt. Savage hunters were extremely careful to protect their souls during the vulnerable transition from a social life ashore to the killing instinct at sea. The shift from one state to another "resembles that of an initiation ritual. The hunter must first prepare and separate himself from society, then encounter and subdue this prey, which requires him to enter into a relationship with an inhabitant of the asocial, natural world, and finally he must return again to human society" (Blackcat, 1988, p.128). Trawlerman Bill O'Pray described his feelings when leaving home for the fish dock, "I used to forget all about the family — once at sea, you were at sea" (2/90).

Anthropological studies may well account for native hunters on Pacific Islands; but it only partly fits Hull's deep-sea trawling industry. In the rational West we have suppressed most old-time rituals. Nevertheless, hunters have universal psychological needs which cannot be easily concealed. I believe that some superstitions are remnants of the hunt magic observed in former times when the taking of fishes lives was respected within a spiritual framework.

The cluster of Hull sailing-day taboos can be seen as a relic of the hunter's initiation ritual of preparing for the kill. The vital 'departing/sailing ritual' survived in Hull (Ch. 1). Then, at the fishing/killing grounds, we saw protective measures with the use of colourful nicknames (Ch. 10). It is less easy to identify the rituals for Hull's trawlermen on their return home. The Blackcat article stated that "the return is often a ritually complex operation...[whereby a fisherman must] purify himself of his relationship with his prey, which is magically dangerous because of its asocial, inhuman and hostile qualities and to protect others from its effects" (Ibid).

It is possible to speculate that the return-home rituals were submerged in the men's long drinking bouts in the company of other men/hunters. Drunkenness was perhaps a way of dealing with the hunter's guilt from having killed and gutted thousands of fish. In the absence of a formal social ritual, the men turned to drink to suppress their deeply hidden feelings.

Another possible way to cope with their subconscious guilt may have been by not talking about their work to outsiders. Mention has been made of the men's tendency to 'never divulge' (Ch. 11). Once ashore, few talked about their trawling experience. The families of some trawlermen know next to nothing about what their fathers work involved at sea. Men who survived a wrecked trawler rarely spoke of their rescue, and war-time memories are also avoided. This is not necessarily because it was too horrific to recount, but more to avoid the risk of seeming boastful of one's achievements. Audrey Grady comments, "you should not get above yourself". Boasting is taboo for a trawlerman. This psycho-social characteristic is yet another feature of the Hessle Road cultural identity. This distinct trawling trait is echoed in the literature: "success in fishing must never be mentioned as this constitutes a form of arrogance that is highly objectionable to the spirits. Greediness amongst fishermen is always unlucky" (Cavendish, 1980, p. 986). This attitude is also reflected in an Old Testament Proverb: "Boast not thyself of tomorrow: For thou knowest not what a day may bring forth. Let another praise thee, not thine own mouth; a stranger and not thine own lips" (Proverbs 27:1). And there is the cliché: 'Pride comes before a fall".

FOOTNOTE: This non-boasting trait partly explains why the British Fishermen's Association's long campaign for justly-deserved redundancy has been ignored by the powers-that-be (Governments, Appeal Courts). The officials are oblivious of the men's daring achievements because there is a tradition of not shouting about them — unlike other industrial groups.

# Chapter 30

## GAMBLER'S LUCK

PROVERB: *They who are afraid of bad luck*
*Will never know good.* (Russian)

Cause and effect can be seen as a chance event. 'Chance' is a posh word for 'Luck'. Rob Ellis, an ex-trawlerman who moved over to the Merchant Navy, made a contrast between the two different mariners: "Fishermen, unlike 'big boat' men, didn't have their cargo on board. They depended on luck to get their cargo from the bottom of the sea".

Mickiko Yusa (1987) stated that "chance denotes human freedom... it can be fortunate or unfortunate. This ambivalence may be traced to the essential unpredictability and unknowability of any occurrence" (p. 192). This academic definition of chance certainly applied to Hull's pre-WWII skippers who had a high degree of freedom to fish the deep-sea waters where and how they wished. Some took more risks than others. The view was "if they got away with it, they were lucky. If not, they paid the price". Trawlermen are natural gamblers. Their croupier is Nature who deals out fog, storms, fire, fish or no fish; other trump cards are collisions, engine failure, sickness, poor markets. All, seemingly, at the hand of Luck. The ancient Roman view was that "we are so much at the mercy of chance that Chance herself takes the place of god" — she being Lady Fortuna — "depicted with wings, bearing a rudder and wheel, symbolising swiftly changing fortune" (Yusa, 1987, p. 194) — the Wheel of Fortune. While the skipper may fear Lady Fortune, his job forced him to challenge her.

Cavendish (1980) stressed that luck has its roots in Nature. Fortuna was originally a rustic deity of fertility, "presumably, the fertility goddess turned into a divinity of luck because successful farming depends so heavily on factors outside the farmer's control" (p. 105). An obvious point to add is that modern farming is less dependent upon the vagaries of Nature since Fortuna's time. But for the trawlermen upon the high seas, Nature is still a dominant force. Sometimes luck is a skipper's only weapon in his war with the elements.

Yet luck is only one side of the gambler's coin. On the darker side is Fate. This topic is oceans deep (Ch. 34). Luck equates well with the free-will argument, while fate is more deterministic. Fate holds that our lives are pre-determined, with no space for chance events. Indeed, the whole 'Luck v. Fate' debate addresses the old cause-and-effect issue — but on a grander scale. Luck is short-term, fate is life-time; luck is good/positive, fate is bad/negative.

Now, although these two views of life are often presented as fighting opposites, there is nevertheless an ironic juxtaposition between these contenders. Total belief in Fate lays itself open to the instruments of chance. If the fatalistic view is true and our lives are strictly laid out, then knowledge of 'what will be' must exist in a book or be mapped out somewhere. Given human curiosity, we desire to find out what destiny holds in store (marriage, children, prospects). This urge to gaze into the crystal ball has generated scores of diverse methods of divination. Central to most is some device to provide a random result. In other words, a chance event (drawing lots, throwing dice, tossing coins, dealing cards). And these in turn pivot upon luck. The underlying belief here is what psychologist Carl Jung called 'synchronicity' — a correspondence between human action and cosmic order. Therefore, even within the labyrinth of Fate can be found a flash of Luck to unlock the pre-determined future. This leads into divination — a practice mirrored within superstition (and an element of the Latin definition of the word 'superstitio' being to 'witness' an event).

*Fishing and gambling overlap. These two prints are fairly unusual. They show trawlermen playing cards on the deck in 1937, and playing dominoes (below) in the mess deck in 1938. By coincidence, both shots were aboard different (un-named) Hudson vessels. In olden times, playing cards were strictly forbidden aboard the sailing ships. They were called the Devil's Bible. A popular pastime amongst the Hull trawlermen was cribbage.*
Courtesy Richard Rilatt and Rennie Acum.

# Chapter 31

## OCCULT OUTLOOK

QUOTE: *What a mother sings to the cradle*
*goes all the way to the coffin.* (Henry B. Ward)

Superstition straddles various systems of belief and occasionally strays into the area of the occult — that supernatural part of life usually 'hidden from view' (Collins).

### READING THE TEA-LEAVES

Sometimes, superstition is divination in disguise. It is an informal way of trying to decipher what Fate holds in store. A few of the endless instances of looking out for omens are: fire gazing, fallen pictures, dropped cutlery, animal watching (birds, cats, rats), broken mirrors, and diamond creases in linen.

Divination is aeons old and practised in most cultures. Anything can be used to divine the future by observing present events. Zuesse (1987) reported many cross-cultural studies which "show that hunting-fishing cultures generally depend on short-term risks and personal initiative, so that individuals are trained from childhood to be self-reliant...individuals possess an encyclopædic knowledge of portents, and of methods for obtaining auguries of the capricious spirits' intentions" (p.377).

As we have seen already with many other aspects of folk magic, "the Jewish and Christian traditions are markedly ambivalent about divination" — with the latter taking the view that it is "demonic and required exorcism". Nevertheless, "a rich and highly varied regional folk practice of divination persisted" (Zuesse, 1987, pp.379-80). His conclusion showed divination in a positive light for people under emotional stress. Because the message is wrapped in vague terms and is open to wide interpretation, it can be grasped more easily. Added to this, the omen has come from an outside source (flying bird) and its random (indirect) nature gives it authority and objectivity (Ch. 26 — Taboo). Given this sign, the widow or whoever can then take confident steps out of a previously confused uncertain depression. Everyday superstition may lead into more formal methods of folk divination: tea-leaf reading, palmistry, astrology, and scrying (gazing into a glass of water).

### FALLING PICTURES

The Hessle Road sub-culture of omens and divination created a climate whereby people were open to premonitions. A premonition is a prior warning of a future event which comes without a conscious search — like a picture falling off the wall in the dead of night. Again the message is indirect, and prompts an instinctive foreboding of a pending disaster. These visions are more inclined to occur to someone in a heightened state of anxiety (pregnancy, during a war, or a wife worried about an overdue trawler).

The link between premonition and superstition is that both involve an awareness of the signs from the world beyond. Often, after I have given a talk about superstitions, some members of the audience confide an incident which involved a premonition. There is a story from the Second World War of a Harrow Street family. Everyone was distressed as they were about to attend their elderly mother's funeral. As they waited for the hearse, a jumper suddenly fell off the washing pulley hung in the living-room, and landed on the shoulders of the man of the house. This seemingly trivial event was seen by some in the family as an ill-omen. The husband subsequently joined his trawler and was lost with everyone else aboard the *Lucida* (A.175) when she was blown up in the North Sea on 11 January 1940.

Another story concerns a woman who was expecting a baby when news came that her brother was lost at sea. Every night while she was carrying, she 'saw' him stood at the foot of her bed. These visitations ceased only after the baby was safely delivered. She concluded, "it was as if he watched over me during that critical time".

In 1931, Alice Saunders pleaded with her son Joseph (29) not to go trawling just before Christmas. The Saunders were not a trawling family and Joe had never been to sea in his life. The family lived in Jackson Street, off Hessle Road. It was because his crane-driving job on the docks was so poorly paid that he desperately needed extra money to buy presents for his three youngsters. His cousin Ted George (23), the youngest Hull skipper, was about to take the *Girdleness* (H.782) trawling on 7th December. He easily got Joe a job as deckhand. The plan was to fish off the Faroes and be home for Christmas —Ted was due to get married then.

A week after Joe sailed off, his mother had a night-mare. She saw her son's body being smashed to pieces on rocks in a stormy sea and heard him cry out to her, "I've been through it". As if that was not enough, Joe's married sister Sarah had a nerve-shattering experience in nearby Madeley Street. For three nights she heard a knocking at their back door. Her family did not believe in premonitions, but this was very spooky. Her husband Charlie Gray was the most sceptical of all — he blamed the neighbours' kids. But even he got the frights in the early hours of one morning. He was tying his boot-laces, getting ready for his coal round, when he heard a loud knocking on the back window. He shouted, "I'll be with you in a minute". But when he went outside into the large yard it was completely empty. This was let to a fish merchant and was securely bolted every night. Sarah, who had a young child, was extremely anxious — "it got on my nerves".

After the third night of Sarah's strange knocking, the *Hull Daily Mail* front-page headline read "Hull Trawler Wrecked off Faroe Islands...Corpses seen floating...Eleven Crew Perish...Grim Yuletide Disaster" (19 Dec. 31). The Saunders felt that the strange knocking had been "a message from Joe that something was going to happen" — a final farewell to his kinfolk before his soul departed. The shock was too much for his family. Mother took it bad and father (50) died within a couple of years.

*Part (a) – Joseph Saunders (29) of Nelson Terrace, Bean Street was lost on his first-ever trawling trip with the **Girdleness** (H.784) just before Christmas on 18 December 1931. Footballer Joe played for the Neptune Inn cup-winning team. At the time of the loss, Joe's mother, Alice, had a nightmare and heard him call, "I've been through it".*

*Part (b) – Prior to this fatal trip, the cook of the **Girdleness**, Arthur Taylor, had the premonition that "there's something about that ship I don't like". Most of the eleven crew were washed ashore at the Faroes and the islanders buried their bodies in a special grave.*
Courtesy Sarah Gray (née Saunders).

Crewmen can develop a peculiar feeling toward a trawler. This was the case with the *Kingston Amber* (H.471). In December 1948 Hull men forced the skipper to put into Lerwick (Shetlands) and nine left the ship (HDM, 15 Dec. 48, p.1). Then, on her next trip, a young deckie-learner suffocated to death during a fire in the fo'c'sle. Four of the crew called the *Amber* an unlucky ship and refused to work. The *Mail* described them as having "a certain attitude" (HDM, 8 Jan. 49. p.1).

It is a tricky area when trying to deal with messages from the dead. One I am not equipped to handle. But the people who do are the Spiritualist Church —these were popular in the Hessle Road community. They satisfied a desperate spiritual thirst which other institutions were reluctant to discuss with the bereaved.


## CONTACTING THE DEAD

During the mid-1930s Elizabeth Groom of Liverpool Street began to dabble in divination. She was looking into a glass of water (scrying) when she 'saw' a leg floating in it. A few days later news came that her husband had had a serious accident when a trawl warp almost severed off his leg at the fishing grounds. Hull doctors could do little for him. Liz next discovered she had the gift of healing. Eventually she got his leg better and he returned to sea. Liz subsequently became a leading Spiritualist in the city. Robert Ramsbottom, whose family has strong fishing ties on both sides, said that many Hessle Roaders went to the meetings "to get a message, especially after forebodings —because there was always the doubt after a loss at sea if their man was dead or alive... most wives saw images of their lost husbands". He claims "All religions preach life after death, but the Spiritualists prove it".

When a trawler was overdue some people went to see a medium like Reg Horton (St. George's Road) or Dorothy Hudson (Saner Street — she registered churches at various addresses over the years) to see if there was any news from the spirits about the crewmen. It was not always the wife, but perhaps her mother, aunt or sister who went on her behalf. It was usually a woman, "you rarely saw a fisherman at these meetings". Although it was a 'woman's thing', whenever she returned home, the men were dying to ask, "Well? What was said then?". If a family in grief had received an ominous message (bird down the chimney), presumably from a man lost at sea, some felt the need to get a more detailed message via a medium.

A special evening was set aside for people to bring along a relative's tie, watch, or cap. Word went around the streets, "Oh! It's Article Night". Dorothy Hudson drew the crowds. Even during a regular service she might suddenly declare, "All stand and sing with me *Eternal Father – 'For Those in Peril on the Sea'*. If there had been no news of a lost trawler, "Everyone got excited with goose-pimples, but worried at the same time — the room buzzed in anticipation, each woman anxious about the pending message".

Jill Harrison went to a Saner Street meeting in 1967 with two friends. She took her lost husband's tie. Tony had been killed in the Christmas Day blaze aboard the *St. Finbarr* (H.308) and his body went down with eleven others when she

*Spiritualist Churches were registered in all sorts of places: parlours, bedrooms, over workshops and, the above, looks as if it is in an old WWII mizzen hut. This Harvest Festival gathering was at The First Spiritualist Church, Gospel Hall, Goodwin Street (c.1950s). The medium was Kate Bentley (née Pounder). This once-outlawed organisation was mainly supported by Hessle Road women who wanted to contact relatives drowned at sea. A body-less bereavement causes untold emotional upset.*
Courtesy Robert Ramsbottom.

sank under tow two days later (Ch. 1). It was an 'Article Night' and Jill placed his tie on the tray as she entered the meeting.

Jill had been before to see Dorothy Hudson, and it had been a laugh that time, but the outcome of this visit was not so funny. In the earlier meeting Jill had placed her front-door key on the tray. The medium said that when Jill got home she, "must open all doors and windows. There is evil in the house and it must be let out". After the three girls left, they had a good giggle. In fits of laughter they, nevertheless, opened all the windows — just in case there was something in what had been said.

But when Tony's tie was picked off the tray by the Spiritualist, Dorothy instantly threw it back down saying, "I don't want to talk about this. It's terrible...blackness!". Jill was shocked by her reaction: Had she seen the black smoke? Equally, she was very sceptical and never went to another meeting.

In addition to these formal services, there were women who acted as clairvoyants, held séances, dealt the tarot cards, or used a Ouija Board to contact the dead. Lily Lee of North Road, Gipsyville, for example, was a fortune-teller. Skippers' wives often paid her a visit. She refused to take any money for her 'folk wisdom', but the women usually left her a gift. The ancient methods used by local women had been handed down from long ago. These practices in the community were not new. They had a parallel within a period we call Pagan.

141

## Chapter 32

## PAGAN PARALLEL

BIBLE: *The thing that hath been,*
*it is that which shall be;*
*And that which is done is that which shall be done;*
*And there is no new thing under the sun.*
(Ecclesiastes 1:9)

In various chapters throughout this book I have suggested that the source of many superstitions can be traced back to Pagan times. This conclusion is repeated here and an attempt is made to draw together different strands of research to support this theory. Within the Pagan period the Celts were a key source, with a Norse influence too. I do not claim any direct, unbroken line from Pagan myth to Hull taboo, but there appears a discernible parallel between the two disparate groups. In essence, the topic of superstition delves into the depths of human thinking — and time seems to have done little to change our instinctive beliefs over the centuries. Many factors contribute to this continuity conclusion.

Animal symbolism was central to Celtic belief and this reflects strongly in Hull's cultural heritage (birds, cats, rats and fish — Part Three). But one creature in particular featured strongly in both the Celtic and the Hessle Road cultures. This is the powerful taboo which surrounds the 'pig'. We saw how grunter was supreme in Pagan mythology (Ch. 18). For the hunting Celts, the wild boar was a sacred being. Equally, in Hull's fishing community it was the pig which caused the greatest reaction of all superstitions. There were nearly one dozen alternatives to avoid its proper name being uttered. And in the hierarchy of beliefs the pig taboo over-ruled other beliefs (if a trawlerman saw a pig while on his way to the fish dock, it would force him to break another strong taboo by 'turning back' and missing his ship — Ch.1).

In addition to the strong parallels between Pagan practice and Hull superstition, there is a historical foundation upon which this link-theory is built. The first is geographical with regard to Yorkshire Celts, and the second is industrial with the founding of Hull's trawling industry by smackmen from S.W. England. And both have a strong connection with pig.

The Celtic tribe which inhabited the East Riding area was the Parisi. Many of their formal burial sites have been excavated north of the Humber Estuary. A familiar feature of these graves is "the frequent occurrence of pig-bones" (Stead, 1979, p.25) — the boars/pigs were sacred in pre-Christian times. Also in the locality of Hull are place names like Swine, and Swanland may have been 'Swine-land' at one time.

The second historical factor comes directly from the fishing industry itself. Hull's trawling did not arise from within the port, but came about as a result of

*The importance of the boar in the culture of the Celts is shown in this Museum illustation by Peter Connolly. The funeral scene of a Parisi nobleman at Wetwang Slack shows the warrior being buried along with his chariot and a wild boar. This sacred animal was seen as a magical creature in the other world. No matter how many times it was killed, cooked or eaten, it always returned the next day to provide a heavenly feast.*
Courtesy Peter Connolly and Hull City Museums & Art Galleries.

a unique migration from outside. Although Hull has centuries of maritime history and a long-established whale fishery — trawling was a fluke event. In brief, it began with the arrival of the Devonshire/Cornish smackmen and their families who settled in increasing numbers from 1843 onwards. Alf Louth is tracing his own fishing family history from Brixham (and that of a smack-owning family who did much to found Hull's trawling heritage). He believes that there are connections between these south-west English families and even earlier Breton family movements from Brittany. As well as the indigenous Parisi roots, I am further suggesting that Celtic traditions were brought into the city when the smack families moved to Hull. It is worth stressing that these outsiders were not welcomed with open arms by the long-established Hull merchants who did much to deny them landing space and encouraged some to move over to Grimsby. Nevertheless, the doggedly independent Breton spirit held out against Yorkshire grit and they stayed — if somewhat isolated. Social distance was further increased because the smack-owners tended to employ workhouse boys as apprentice lads. Barriers of resentment were erected by the locals against the outsiders. The 'foreigners' from down south were strange "fishermen who refused to carry pork to sea" (Opie & Tatem, 1989, p.307).

The pork/pig taboo is difficult to explain. It is, however, possible to speculate that the pig was the subconscious totem animal of the Hessle Roaders. Animal symbolism is still common even today. The totem creature of Britain is the bull-dog (and lion) — a useful national emblem during a time of war; and Hull's three major sports teams are each represented by a totem animal: Hull City Tigers, Hull F. C. Airlie Birds, and Hull Kingston Robins. At the fishing community level I believe that the feared boar (or cunning pig) is the symbolic totem of the Hessle Roaders. This is not such a far-fetched idea when we recall that various British aristocratic families' heraldic shields depict the boar as their totem symbol — especially in Wales, Scotland and Ireland. Support for this theory is based upon Freud's (1913) *Totem and Taboo* book. He stated that "the totem animal protects and gives warning to members of its clan... foretells the future... and serves as a guide... sometimes [clan members] are forbidden to touch it, or even look at it; in a number of cases the totem may not be spoken of by its proper name. Any violation of the taboos that protect the totem are automatically punished by severe illness or death" (pp.101-104).

In addition to the boar, the Celts wove many legends around fish and birds. These and other creatures were central in divination. The Celts were continually on the look out for signs from their gods and messages from deceased kin (Ch. 16). And were in awe of tree spirits and sea gods. The trawlermen who superstitiously threw coins into the estuary and fishing grounds re-enacted the paying of a sacrifice to the pagan gods (Ch. 25).

Another Celtic-Hessle Road parallel involves the oral tradition. Superstitions pass from one generation to another by word of mouth. They do not come from scripture or by rote learning. They were handed on by the durable technique favoured by the Celts. The Druids forbade any written record of their rituals or beliefs. This is not to say they were illiterate. When it came to trade with other cultures, they sometimes wrote in Greek (Ross, 1980, p.439). They firmly believed that *words* have power — an idea as old as the first utterance (Ch. 12). The vast number of taboo words and avoidance of one's own name (use of nicknames) gives testimony to this practise being continued in Hull (Ch. 10). Anne Ross (1980) stated, "the Celts believed it was undesirable and positively dangerous to name a sacred thing by its correct name. As a result, the gods are often referred to in a roundabout way" (p.443). The numerous alternative names for animals and objects reflected this roundabout (indirectness) in 20th century Hull. The oral tradition was an effective form of learning. No one overtly taught children superstitions — they were picked up unwittingly (indirectly). They were not part of any school time-table. They were passed on verbally. Perhaps the secret of their effectiveness was in the latent threat of bad luck (and a clip on the ear) which might befall any guilty party. This *'fear of the gods'* element may explain the once-and-for-all impact the taboos have on the human mind. The survival of these Celtic ways is even more remarkable when we consider the centuries of mockery, derision and even torture levelled against the superstitions by priests and scientists. Yet they not only survive, but thrive without any written tradition.

The Pagan roots of the superstitions go a long way to explain why the Church is antagonistic toward taboos. This poles-apart rift between the two belief systems is reflected in the tradition that "it is unlucky to meet a clergyman when setting off to sea" (Ch. 9). A related point is that the ancient Celts "did not as a rule build formal temples" — they tended to use more natural settings of sacred springs, wells, trees or copse (Ross, 1980, p.440). Likewise, few fishing families were regular church-goers. This does not mean they were heathens. It is just that their ways did not necessarily conform to the Christian pattern of formal worship.

A further parallel is that the Celts "tended to express things in an oblique fashion abhorring direct statement and...preferring the subtle allusion, the hint" (Ross, 1980, p.440). This aspect finds an echo in the Hessle Roaders preference "not to divulge" and to avoid boasting about their achievements — so as 'not to tempt Fate' — or 'get above themselves' (Ch. 11 & 29).

The face-to-face confrontation with Nature is another bond between the Celtic/Nordic peoples and the 20th century trawlermen. This point is self-evident with deep-sea fishing. The comparisons between these peoples are that they were hunters/fishers, took chances, relied upon luck, carried protective charms, risked their lives, lived close to death, and grief and guilt were part of daily living. Simons (1973), in his first chapter 'The Nature of Superstitions', stated that "in its inception, superstition sprang from man's helplessness in the face of Nature. He created ritual and taboo to shield him from the hostile forces all around: magic...became the key to an understanding of natural processes" (p.4).

Lightning looms large in the imagination of both the Pagans and the Hessle Roaders. Sir James Frazer (1922) dedicated the concluding sections of his life-long work, *Study in Magic and Religion*, to the mythological ways in which the Celts were awe-struck by lightning. He conjectured that "the Druids worshipped a mistletoe-bearing oak...in the belief that it had been struck by lightning... [and by various] mystical rites they were securing for themselves all the magical properties of a thunder-bolt" — thus Frazer titled his book *The Golden Bough* (p.710). And in the 20th century, we saw the legends built around St. Elmo's fire — little flashes of ethereal light which danced around the trawler's mast and rigging (Ch. 25). And ashore, more dramatically, how women behaved at home during an electric storm with the frantic covering of mirrors and hiding away of the family silver so that lightning would not strike indoors (Ch. 21). Violent thunder and lightning is frightening. It is easy to see how our primitive ancestors would personify this natural phenomena as the gods in a rage of anger. I would therefore suggest that the lightning-related superstitions are a clear illustration of the *'fear of the gods'* definition in action (Ch. 26).

Fire sometimes follows lighting and this too provides yet a further similarity. The Celts were fond of fire festivals, especially Beltane to celebrate 1st May (now Labour/Worker's Day). Equally, there is evidence of fire magic in the Hessle Road community in the way women watched for 'strangers on the bar' and how a flying spark protected a trawler lost at sea (Ch. 21). In a more grisly vein, the green-aversion is accounted for in terms of the Druids who locked criminals in cages of entwined branches to sacrifice 'green men' as a burnt offering to the gods of vegetation — 'ashes to ashes' (Ch. 23).

Salt and iron are other natural elements which form a common bond

*Sarah Elizabeth Taylor of No. 76 Manchester Street was one of the many Hessle Road women described as 'Fay' – having second-sight – "She could see through brick walls". On 1 February 1917 she walked into her front-room and saw the lips move on a photograph of her son-in-law Henry Brown. Sarah heard him say the name of his wife 'Laura'. She stood rigid and screamed aloud, "Oh! God". Within a few days news came from his regiment that he had been killed in France – not in action, but kicked to death by an army mule he had taken for watering. Sarah is here with her husband Harry (c.1910).*
Courtesy Marion Toffolo.

between these two diverse groups. Anne Ross (1980) wrote about the Celts that "the people grew rich through mining and trading in salt, a most valuable commodity in the ancient world. The chieftains used iron instead of bronze for their weapons, thereby improving their chances in warfare" (p.439). An affinity with these two natural materials was found in superstitions about 'spilling salt' and 'touching cold iron' (Ch. 22 & 25). Again, Pagan myth was perpetuated through modern superstition.

I would like to add to this Pagan section a quote from Kathleen Raine's (1985) book *Defending Ancient Springs*: "The myths of all races are timeless, since their symbolic language is based upon the permanent and unchanging elements of the world we inhabit" (p.119). In effect, the Hessle Roaders are torch-bearers of the ancient folk myths which still burn in the hearts of the ordinary people. Flashes of the ageless legends flickered in their everyday superstitions. In this noble sense, Hull's fishing families can be seen as Urban Pagans who kept alive universal beliefs. Their taboos reflect the unchanging human emotions experienced by the Celtic and Nordic peoples. This perpetual theme is continued with a topic that requires a chapter to itself — the historical female influence on Hull's superstitious heritage.

# Chapter 33

## WOMAN:
### Wicked or Wise?

PROVERB: *Every woman has something
of a witch about her.* (Spanish)

Hidden behind many seafaring taboos is the figure of woman. Various Hull superstitions pivot upon the male-female relationship. The often-absent crewman, in many ways, led a distinctly separate life from his wife (both had their own social network and life-pattern). A cluster of superstitions seem to have an anti-woman tone: women not allowed to whistle, a cross-eyed woman was bad luck, a woman could not first-foot on New Year's Day, an unchurched mother was shunned, and some said she was 'unclean', especially if she gave birth to a girl. But the severest restrictions placed on women came with the sailing-day taboos: not washing, waving, going on dock, or being allowed to set foot on a trawler.

In view of this range of restrictions, I have pondered whether the male attitude toward women was one of antagonism or not? Either way the superstitions seem to reflect an unconscious ambivalence — awful or awesome? The word 'awe' is chosen deliberately because it means: 'great fear mingled with veneration and apprehension of danger... to inspire with awe... majestic' (Collins). We continue the pre-historic search to find a possible answer to this question of where woman stood when viewed through the eyes of superstition.

Goddess worship dates back to the birth of time. Indeed, this strand of the research goes into the pre-Celtic period of the New Stone Age (Neolithic). Goddess figurines have been traced to around 40,000 years ago — but "they appear more frequently abut 25,000 BC". For every one male figure found, there are ten depicting a female. This vast quantity from every inhabited continent is beginning to disprove the previously dismissive male attitude which wrote them all off as "mere fertility symbols". Preston (1987) highlighted their wide diversity and claimed that, "these figures may have been associated with pregnancy, birth, burial, fertility, initiation, hunting, and the menstrual cycle; and may even have had some erotic function". The Goddess is often portrayed in cave paintings as partially animal — a snake or a bird, and in some regions a fish-woman. One of her forms associated with death is the boar. In a Neolithic site in south Turkey, she "has command over wild animals".

A few goddess names from world-wide cultures are Isis (Egypt), Kali (India), Tara (China), Amaterasu (Japan), Demeter and Gaia (Greece), al-Uzzā (Arabia), Asheráh (Canaan), Frigg (Scandinavia), Cybele and Diana (Italy). Many are shown as triple goddesses — sometimes as the trinity of maiden, mother and crone, which harmonise with the three phases of the moon: new, full and old — a cycle of Nature which regenerates herself. These goddesses characterise not just life-giving and healing qualities, but also the darker powers of a violent and vengeful deity who demands blood sacrifice and death. Preston concluded that goddess worship extends "deep into antiquity and continues to thrive in many of the world's religions even today" (pp. 35-45).

The transition from the worship of goddesses to the pre-eminence of a sole male god took centuries (between the 10th and 6th centuries BC). But as Stone (1987) pointed out, "in the lands that brought forth Judaism, Christianity, and Islam, God was once worshipped in the form of woman" — Asheráh the 'Mother of the Deities' (p.48). After this switch in emphasis came the degradation of woman. A prime example is Eve being blamed for Man's banishment from the Garden of Eden. Just as most newly-elected political parties blame its ills on the previous government, so it was when the male god deposed the many female goddesses.

The ceaseless denigration of woman persisted over the centuries. It culminated in the European witch hunts which saw countless thousands (some say millions) of women who were persecuted and executed. All the darker characteristics of the former goddesses were emphasised and projected onto non-conforming women who clung to some of the old Pagan remedies and superstitions.

*Nordic Goddess Frigg at her Fensalir Palace spinning the clouds of the sky. Ann Dunnigan (1987) wrote that "the goddesses Aphrodite, Venus and Frigg were assimilated to fish, and on Friday –the day sacred to them – fish was eaten as a way of participating in their fecundity" (p.346). Pagan fishermen, therefore, were afraid to set sail on the holy day dedicated to such powerful female goddesses. The French name for Friday is Vendredi – after Venus. Friday is the only day of the week named after a woman.*
Courtesy Freya Cross.

The fearful figure of a witch-like woman has even been mentioned during my interviews. When researching the life of Midwife Julia Turpin — who lived and worked in the community until her death in 1936 (Gill, 1991, Ch. 2) — one of her relatives bluntly described her as "a bit of a witch...who laid down the law in her family... like a dragon... with her big black medicine bag, and her house full of old books with ancient remedies". Added to this, Midwife Turpin was a keen Spiritualist at the Dairycoates Mission — thus mixing mystery with her wise ways. For every medically-trained midwife there were scores of local wise women — practically one in each terrace. A healer like Granny Gadie is one example. She knew the home-spun remedies (others practised herbalism,) and freely gave medical advice at times of illness in the neighbourhood. She also prepared a woman for confinement and helped with the delivery. Most terrace midwives tended to be middle-aged, the one to whom a younger mum turned to for advice when her child was seriously ill and the family could not afford to pay for a doctor to visit. Equally, when death hovered, the local midwife was sent for to sit by the bed of a dying relative. When the inevitable happened, she knew how to lay out the body before rigor mortis stiffened the bones of the deceased. She knew what to do in the critical areas of life, sickness and death —'knowledge is power'.

Myths about witches are universal. It is useful to draw them together to see how they gave rise to a variety of the superstitions found in Hull. This condensed image is based upon a Time-Life book by Brendan Lehane (1984) called *Wizards and Witches* in a chapter entitled 'The Shadowy Sisterhood' (pp.97-141). He stated that there are both black witches and white ones — in continuous battle between evil and good. The black witch sold her soul to Satan in exchange for magical powers. Even a husband may be unaware that his wife is a cunning witch.

Through sympathetic magic she has power over the elements and controls the weather, especially at sea by whistling up the wind, stirring up a storm, and bringing down thunder and lightning from the heavens (Ch. 4). She can shift her shape into that of any animal, such as a hare, crow, dog, snake, or raven (Ch. 16). Her best-known familiar, though, is the black cat which is why this creature attracted so many taboos. The curiosity being that trawlermen welcomed a cat aboard and did not reject her like fishermen the world over (Ch. 17). The wicked witch is seen as a serious threat to everyone, especially babies before baptism, and anyone's health can be crippled at a glance (Ch. 3). But the worst threat from her Evil Eye is to make a man impotent or a mother miscarry (Ch. 5). She has the ability to fly on a broomstick, but we encountered her little-known sailing skills with eggshells. Children were urged, after eating a boiled egg, to break the empty shell to prevent a witch using it as a boat to cause havoc at sea and wreck ships (Ch. 22).

Folk myth tells us that ordinary people are susceptible to witchcraft at critical 'in-between' times. Midnight falls between one day and the next, so that is when her imagined power is at its height; likewise with the full moon, between the wax and wane. Threateningly for Hull trawlermen, she is most menacing at high tide — between the flow and ebb of the Humber, thus the array of protective rituals of the sailing-day superstitions (Ch.1). This shows up superstitiously by a woman not being allowed on the dockside at high tide or aboard a trawler about to set sail, just in case she was a devious witch able to cast an evil spell on the ship (Ch. 6). Equally, at births and funerals she hovers between life and death (Ch. 3 & 14). The equinox and solstice are her times too — thus the range of New Year rituals (Ch. 24).

Other malicious methods of the black witch include the casting of spells and charms by the use of magic words and incantation to bewitch the innocent in her neighbourhood (especially if she can get hold of hair or nail cuttings — Ch. 5). Divination is another art (Ch. 31). She magically peers into the fixed future by the use of mirrors, fire sparks, knives, and cards — the Devil's Bible (Ch. 21). In summary, the unconscious fear of the wicked witch, secretly at work in the close-knit fishing community, under-pinned many superstitions.

Within this shadowy context, protection against black magic is not easy for an ordinary family. As a defence against imagined curses and spells, an anxious mother may turn to a good-natured terrace midwife for guidance. As well as Turpin and Gadie, there were other family names associated with midwifery in Hessle Road: Cavill, Fozard, Harrington, Lister, Randall, Skelton, Stark, and Waddington, Some of their mothers had moved into Hull's fishing community during the decades of expansion (1850/1890). They came to the port from rural areas where they had been 'village midwives' conversant with the old cures, healing ways and homely remedies of the white witch.

Some administered herbal remedies and used magic methods, including divination by opening up the Holy Bible at random. Others may have given advice about protective materials such as salt (placed in cradles or sprinkled on unlucky nets — Ch. 22), iron (in the shape of a lucky horse-shoe — Ch. 25), a baby's caul (to prevent drowning — Ch. 2), mid-summer plants and garlic, or gave a lucky talisman (Ch. 25). Word magic would be stressed to ward off bad luck by avoiding taboo utterances, and use of protective words such as White Rabbit, Cold Iron, and Touching Wood (Ch. 8-12). Margaret Murray (1921) argued in her book *The Witch-Cult in Western Europe* that witchcraft was not an anti-Christian perversion, but simply a *survival* of pre-Christian paganism (Blackcat, 1988, p.20). It seems that some of the Celtic crafts were kept alive by the village women in tune with the oral transmission of the ancient wise ways.

We can now return to the question of male-female relationships in the community as seen from the perspective of the superstitions. The trawlermen's ambivalence toward women reflected the fact that Celtic/Pagan practices persist in a Christian country (Ch. 32). The women held true to the older wisdom, while the men wavered between the two conflicting belief systems. This male dilemma is described by Radford (1974): "In case of the seamen's superstitions, there may also be traces of Christianity's early days, when many had a foot in both camps; acknowledging Christ on shore, but still putting the old gods first when out on the perilous sea" (p.104). In other words, they placed an each-way bet because they were not sure who was right.

The notion of the Celtic thread being kept alive by women is supported by Abrahams (1894). He theorised about the Celtic people of Flamborough (a small fishing village on the Yorkshire coast) when the Angles invaded Britain (c.440 AD). He expressed the view that "it is generally supposed that the conquerors killed or drove away most of the men...and appropriated the women. Hence a good many articles used by the women have old British or Celtic names" (p.2) — and, no doubt, their old folk wisdom also continued and was passed on verbally by the women to their sons and daughters.

Within the busy Hessle Road community a swirl of mystery eddied around the 'ways of woman'. She was open to omens, felt forebodings, delved into divination, was prone to premonitions, and attended Spiritualist meetings with friends. The weird fire-side messages, tea-leaf reading, fortune-telling and talk of fallen pictures disturbed some of the trawlermen. Word magic is powerful. Female intuition can unnerve a man.

This female-male rift was further widened by ignorance about the menstrual cycle — the monthly 'curse' which caused some women to have unpredictable mood swings. The fact that it is somehow controlled by the mysterious moon only deepens the confusion. This triggers off other subconscious associations with moon-goddesses like Frigg (Friday), lunacy, and control over the tides (Ch. 24). "In primitive societies women are subject to special taboos and restrictions during their monthly period" (Walker, 1977, p.170). She is charged with a powerful supernatural energy during that time. And "her presence in a boat is said to raise storms" (Frazer, 1922, p.606). Walker claimed that this mystery surrounding the woman's cycle was "the foundation of all taboos and initiation rites. Here girls were taught the secrets of the feminine functions, the fertility rituals...love magic, including the use of herbs and poisons. This secrecy...may have aroused the sex envy of the male and caused him to adopt his own 'mysteries' and initiations, in imitation of the exclusive female rites" (p.171). Thus, the growth of 'men only' groups such as the Masons, Buffaloes, working-men's clubs, and a wall of superstition which forbade women on a Hull trawler (Ch. 6).

While a man was away at sea the woman was 'mother and father both to their children'. In his absence, she established a close matriarchal network of female contacts: grannies, her mother, in-laws, aunts, sisters, daughters — plus her friends and neighbours. When a young woman was due to marry, her mother spoke to the rent collector to see if a house was coming empty in her terrace. Thus, kinship clusters lived in the same area. The noted 'community spirit' of Hessle Road stemmed more from the inter-action of the women than the men who were away at sea for most of the time (approximately 9-10 months over a year).

An ulterior motive for many of the superstitions which restricted what the women could and could not do may, indeed, be the product of the absent males' jealousy. There was an unwritten law that "a fisherman's wife did not go out to work". He was the bread-winner and if he could not provide for her, it reflected badly upon his manhood. Added to this, he wanted her at home, no matter what tide he landed, to provide for his physical and sexual needs. Underlying all this, however, was that if she went out to work she would mix with men and it would be easy for her to be unfaithful. That is why net-braiding at home was so popular. She earned extra money without leaving the house.

One negative effect of the superstitions which shackled a woman is that some were permanently affected by guilt after a trawling tragedy. Women have confided their misgivings and self-blame for having waved her husband off, or quarrelled the day he sailed. The weight of this guilt is both heavy and long-lasting — 25 years and the anguish is sometimes still untouched and unresolved.

The guilt is needless because sympathetic magic is unfounded. Mary O'Neil (1987) concluded her article about 'Superstitions' by stating that magical beliefs and practice make misplaced assumptions about causality stemming from a faulty understanding of nature and "the impossibility of magical effects in a universe governed by natural law" (p.165). Even Frazer (1922) pointed out that, "Homoeopathic [mimic] magic commits the mistake of assuming that things which resemble each other are the same; and contagious [touch] magic commits the mistake of assuming that things which have once been in contact with each other are always in contact" (p.12). In other words, a woman who 'waves' does not cause a 'wave' to wash her husband overboard (Ch. 1). And the sister who 'washed' on New Year's Day did not 'wash' her brother away two weeks later (Ch. 24). It is, therefore, unnecessary for any woman to carry this burden. The guilt, however, is a by-product of the superstitions. But this is not the purpose of the fishing taboos — as we will see (Ch. 34).

I began this chapter by pondering if the trawlermen's attitude toward women was one of favour or fear. Within the Pagan-goddess light it was positive; but in the post-Christian period woman has been placed in a sinister shade. This dual role caused ripples in the Hull fishing community — a phenomena which seems universal in a hunting culture. Simons (1973) claimed that "sometimes women are seen as representing a generalised danger and men in some primitive societies try to steer clear of them before setting out on a hunting or fishing expedition" (p.6).

Regardless of culture, there has emerged a pattern in mythology whereby three women appear together. This strong female trinity rules the affairs of mortal men — whether they like it or not. These ladies are the Three Fates. "The prehistoric Great Goddess survives still in folklore. She appears as Fate (or sometimes as three Fates) who attends the birth of a child and foretells the length of its life" (Gimbutas, 1987, p.511). It is within this additional woman-related topic that we begin to establish the real function of the superstitions amongst Hull's trawling families.

# Chapter 34

## 'DON'T TEMPT FATE'

PROVERB: *The sea is a woman.*
*The sea is wonderful.*
*Her other name is Fate.*

A major conclusion of this book is that the Hull superstitions bred into the fishing families a high degree of fatalism. Fate and Fortune are both seen as feminine. Before we examine how Fate was threaded into the trawling tapestry, we will take a brief look at how fatalism itself has evolved.

The three female Fates have fallen from favour since their grand Greek beginnings. Gillian Edwards (1974) has an opening chapter called 'Fates and Fays' in which she traced the history of the pagan goddesses Clotho, Lachesis, and Atropos. They preside over the course of human life: the birth, its span, and when it will be cut down. Once, they were dominant figures whom "the Gods themselves had no power to set aside their decrees". Yet the three ended up as tiny fairy creatures forced to flee underground. Edwards wrote "Goddesses who possess it [power] were both loved and feared. And when it couldn't eradicate their worship, Christianity all too often proclaimed that they were devils, thirsty for souls" (p.7). Yet the ordinary folk and creative poets refused to let these fatal sisters go. They appear time and again in children's fairy tales, in the Arthurian legend as Morgan le Fay, as Shakespearian characters (Midsummer Night's Dream), and as enchanting sirens who lure sailors to their death.

It seems unlikely that the average Arctic trawlerman was well versed in the Greek classics. But he would not need to be. The pervasive trio infiltrated most cultural attitudes. In Scandinavia they were The Norns — three sisters (Urd, Verdandi and Shield) who wove the web of fate. They were consulted by the gods, had the power of divination and knew when our end was nigh (Guerber, 1908, pp.165-72). In their poetic garb they are the Fates; but when this same mental outlook is in its philosophical gown it is known as Fatalism. This profound view of life is the one most readily adopted by many Hessle Roaders. Indeed, deep fatalism is firmly anchored in the fishing superstitions.

This philosophy of life is illustrated with a batch of inter-related trawling superstitions which I have deliberately held back until now. Considering that the trawlermen's livelihood came from the sea, it is curious that there was a 'never-learn-to-swim' superstition. When this taboo is questioned, the general response is "why prolong the agony?". This makes some sense in the wintry Arctic waters. A trawlerman plunged into the sea froze to death before there was time to be drowned. The shock of the sub-zero temperature collapsed the lungs. Nevertheless, this non-swimming belief is extremely defeatist in the calmer summer-time waters of the North Sea when it might be feasible to swim over to a nearby life-belt and be saved. When questioned further, crewmen add a related belief which only makes sense within a superstitious context: "If a man is saved, the sea will simply claim someone else". This is the crux of this book. It is Fatalism in action. This profound aspect is reflected in various real-life tales.

In the mid-1930s, trawler mate Fred Noble, while getting the catch inboard was swept into the sea by a wave. As he bobbed about helplessly in the foam, the skipper reached out and grabbed him. The mate was pulled back from the edge of a watery grave. The sea gods were cheated of their human sacrifice. On his next voyage that same skipper was washed overboard and disappeared forever. The sea gods got their revenge. Philippa Waring (1978) summed up this universal superstition: "Perhaps the cruellest belief — and it still persists in some parts of the world — is that one should never attempt to rescue a drowning person for if it is the will of the water gods that the person should die and if they are defied, then the rescuer himself must expect to fill the same role at a later date" (p. 81). The sea god is personified as a voracious being who demands a sacrifice in human life. After all, the fishermen take their living from the sea, so it is not unnatural that a price be paid: "Ask not the price of fish, for it is paid in men's lives" (Anon). And the sons of Hull fatalistically paid that price over the decades.

The *Hull Daily Mail* (11 Mar. 33) described how "Cruel Fate" dealt a heavy blow to the family of Ernest Parkes (21). He was bosun of the *Dunnet* (H.77) sailing with his brother — the skipper. They had only recently lost their father who skippered the *Endon* (H.161) which sank that January (Ch.7). Ernest would have been lost with his dad, but took a trip off to sit an exam for his mate's ticket. The Parkes family was spared a double loss for the time being. But when Ernie sailed aboard the *Dunnet*, third hand Webb had an accident and was bleeding to death after a serious head injury. Ernie and deckhand Featherstone (who also missed the fatal trip with the *Endon*) got Webb into a coggie-boat to row him over to the hospital ship. No sooner had they left the ship's side when a heavy sea overturned their small craft. All three plunged into the wild sea and were swept away. They were too numb to reach out for life-lines thrown to them. Both Parkes and Featherstone, who seemed to defy the sea by not going on the *Endon*, were taken by it on their next trip.

Cyril Kenyon (21) was another man, apparently, marked out by the wicked sea. Four days after leaving Hull aboard the *St.Neots* (H.112) he was washed overboard and lost. His father was the ship's bosun. The *Mail* article made the ironic point that Cyril had been washed overboard from the same trawler during the previous year — but on that occasion he was rescued (10 Mar. 27). The implicit message is that there is 'no escape from Fate'.

For the women too, Fate could deal a bitter blow. Edna Leake describes how she was made "an orphan as a result of the First World War and a widow in the Second". History repeated itself in that the tragedy which befell her mother also struck Edna. Her father, Charlie Drury, was lost aboard the *Scotland* (H.348) sunk by a WWI mine still floating around in the North Sea on 7 March 1919. Edna was only four-years old. She subsequently married Mack Leake who, in April 1941, worked aboard the *Commander Horton* (H.233) — this was his final trip before joining the Royal Navy. His trawler was also struck by a German mine off the coast of Iceland (Ch. 1). So fate dealt this second blow to Edna's family — she was left to bring up her two boys alone, as well as looking after her widowed mother. An uncanny irony is that Edna was 26-years old —exactly the same age when her mother was made a widow. Very hard to explain, other than by Fate.

Another tale from the war-torn community is told by the Futty family. In accounting for his 47-year old father's death, Stan said "I think it is just coincidence — if it has to happen it will — it's Fate, isn't it? Dad just changed shifts and was killed in an air-raid in 1941. If your number is on it, you'll get it. Life is planned for you".

But Fate does not just have evil plans — it has a kind side too — and trawlermen were sometimes spared. One such example comes from a non-swimmer rescued from the *Edgar Wallace* (H.262) on 9 January 1935 in the fast-flowing Humber. For hours Bill Cameron clung to the ship's wireless mast. It just snapped the instant he was rescued. He was only one of three who survived from a crew of eighteen.

The next sentence is almost a cliché in Hull because, once started, there is always a majority in most audiences who will finish it off: "There's many a trawlerman been washed overboard by one wave... " and they complete it by adding, "...and washed back again by another". The simple fatalistic explanation of this is, "Their time had not yet come". The sea gods did not want them, so their soul was spared. The sea had taken its quota, and so these men were given back to their families. It is also not long before some member of the audience tells of a trawlerman washed back twice. But the story of George Drewery is of a man cast overboard three times and lived. He died at the grand old age of 77 — good going for a skipper.

His short *Fishing News* obituary (May 91) referred to his "three close encounters with death". I went to interview his wife Liz (née Oliver) to fill in the gaps (4/93). George's first lucky escape came aboard H.M.T. *Rutlandshire* (GY.335) mine-sweeping in a fjord during the blunder-ridden Norwegian campaign. She was torpedoed at Namsos on 20 April 1940. George was one of the fortunate survivors who was pulled out of the icy water. His second scrape with death is described by his brother-in-law Laurie Oliver. George was mate of the *Balthazar* (H.359) off the notorious Nord Cap of Iceland in the late 1940s "and he was on the deck when a big sea came aboard, picked him up and swept him clean overboard. Before he hardly knew what had happened another wave picked him up and chucked him back on board again" (Popham, 1957, pp. 102-3).

George's third "and most remarkable escape" came around 1951 when he was skipper of the *Tesla* (H.573) during a severe storm. Instead of sending his radio spark to fix a damaged aerial, 'Free 'n Easy' George clambered on top of the wheel-house himself. Drewery lost his footing and was in the drink for the third time. The mate of the *Tesla* was George Oliver — another brother-in-law. He searched and searched though knew the chances were slim of finding the skipper alive. For the sake of his sister Liz Drewery, the mate desperately wanted to find George's body at least. Then something in the distance caught

*Luck is not evenly spread. Skipper George Drewery seemed to have had more than his fair share of good fortune. Three times in his trawling life he was rescued from the seas. Unlike many fishermen, George was a very good swimmer. He also had musical talent as seen above with his ukelele in his pre-WWII days [the original print is badly damaged]. He also spoke fluent Latin and French, and played piano in the pubs. When he retired from the sea he even turned his hand to computing.*
Courtesy Liz Drewery & Carol Coiffait.
*The **Tesla** (H.573 – below) fishing off Greenland in September 1949. It was from this trawler that George had his third and most miraculous rescue from the sea (a couple of years later).*
Courtesy Kathleen Gray.

his eye which triggered off a gut feeling. In the middle of nowhere a group of seabirds hovered around. Whenever birds see a corpse afloat they peck at the eyes. Oliver ordered full steam ahead and steered directly towards the squawking seabirds. Skipper Drewery was there. The crew got his frozen body aboard. After twenty minutes in the water there was barely a glimmer of life in him. For nearly half-an-hour the mate gave George artificial respiration until he re-gained consciousness. He was landed at Iceland for hospital treatment and later flown home. George Drewery was more than lucky. The Three Fates (or sea gods) certainly favoured him.

One of my most touching interviews was with Minnie Eddom (11/87) — the mother of Harry who was the sole survivor of the terrible tragedy when three Hull trawlers were lost in 1968 — he was mate of the *Ross Cleveland* (H.61). When Minnie was flown out to Iceland to see Harry in hospital, local newspapers dubbed her '*The Miracle Boy's Mother*'. The one question I was burning to ask was, "Why do you feel your son was the only man to live when 58 others died?". Her thoughtful answer was, "Fate. It's allotted out for us... you won't go before your time". In reflecting upon this 1968 time of sadness, Hull City Councillor Kath Green commented, "Fathers went to sea, sons followed — it was in their blood. They always knew that when they went away, especially in winter, they might never be seen again" (8/84). This fact was at the heart of the fishing community: The Hull trawlermen (and kinfolk) lived with death all the time.

I once asked twice-saved Clarrie Wilcockson (89), another of the three survivors of the turned-turtle *Edgar Wallace*, "Did the crewmen panic when the trawler was going down?". After a brief pause he looked at me and said, "No. Trawlermen are not the type to get excited in danger — they are *always* in danger". (Gill, 1991, p.42). This profound answer gives a deep insight into the serious side of the community's superstitions. It provides the major reason for the existence of the wide range of fishing taboos. The overall purpose and outcome of the superstitions is to breed within each fishing family a high degree of fatalism.

Fatalism is, after all, the most appropriate philosophy when confronted by relentless Nature. It is suited to those who live a perilous life-style. It provides the simplest way to account for sudden inexplicable loss of life (sometimes on a massive scale), or the miraculous sparing of life. Likewise for the widows at home. Fatalism does not necessarily ease the grief (made more prolonged and painful due to the absence of a body), but it accelerates the acceptance of the loss and enables the woman to come to terms with her plight. Although on one hand, the superstitious families do all they can to avert bad luck, once that protection has gone and the inevitable is unavoidable, there is a calm acceptance of death — fatalism takes over.

This point is illustrated by the calm acceptance displayed by at least four Hull skippers on doomed trawlers when each stared death in the face. Skipper T.A. Enevoldson (66) was on the bridge of the *Lord Deramore* (H.461) with his son Harold on the 5 March 1933. They were steaming home from the White Sea grounds when they ran into a violent gale off Vardo, North Norway at 1.30 a.m. This respected skipper had pioneered the Russian waters off Murmansk, and was very popular in Hull. Crewmen found it difficult to pronounce his Danish first name (Thyge), so they fondly nicknamed him 'Charlie Teager'. In blinding snow the *Deramore* struck rocks and heeled over quickly.

The four engineers were trapped below, but everyone else had time to abandon ship. Charlie saw the remaining ten men into the life-boat, but he had no intention of joining them. He would not leave his ship, nor those trapped in the engine-room. In the raging storm, his son Harold had to be restrained in the life-boat. He frantically tried to leap overboard to rescue his father. The last time the crew saw their skipper he was stood on the wheelhouse veranda. As the trawler disappeared from their view, Enevoldson was simply heard to shout out to his men, "Good Luck".

The *Lorella* (H.455) and *Roderigo* (H.135) both capsized within a few hours of each other in a severe blizzard on 26 January 1955 off NW Iceland. In a chapter called 'Black Frost', Alan Villiers (1956) described this disaster in his book *Posted Missing*. He recorded how, "still in Skipper Blackshaw's quiet voice, the *Lorella* was heard to say, 'I am going over now. Going over', the voice repeated, as if the speaker were going over to a comfortable home" (p. 102). After she disappeared forever, a USAF pilot got into radio contact with Skipper George Coverdale of the *Roderigo* to ask, "What are your intentions?". The Hull man's calm and accepting reply was "No intentions. Going further over. No visibility. Still going over to starboard...". Then, by morse-code, the simple words "Still going over" were repeated time and time again until the air-waves fell silent.

A similar ring of acceptance came across in the final words of Skipper Phil Gay as the *Ross Cleveland* was blown over in Isafjord on 4 February 1968. He calmly said, "I am going over. Give my love and the crew's love to their wives and families... " and the ship became an iron coffin in a watery grave. The sole survivor being Harry Eddom mentioned earlier.

Surviving, indeed, is a vital aspect of life in Hull's perilous trawling industry, and a major reason why the Hessle Road culture was drawn to such a superstitious outlook. Psychologist Jahoda (1969) concluded his final chapter about 'The Future of Superstitions' by saying "in situations of acute danger or distress: usually involving excessive uncertainty, superstition is particularly likely to come to the fore... [while] at the same time... giving the person at least the feeling of having some control; although illusory, this may well help to preserve the integrity of the personality" (p. 146). He dismissed the many people who "cherish the illusion that superstition is gradually fading away". And his final sentence claimed that superstition "can never be eradicated because, paradoxically, it is an integral part of the adaptive mechanisms without which humanity would be unable to survive" (p. 147).

Looked at pragmatically, to panic at the moment of death does not help. Indeed, it only makes a bad situation worse. Again, the men's life-time of being socialised by family superstitions conditioned into them a deep respect for the cruel side of Mother Nature in which life or death are either side of the same spinning coin.

There is an inner logic to the way in which those who pitch themselves against the might of Nature, who chance their luck with the elements, who cheekily defy Lady Fortune, who gamble against the odds, who push their luck to the limit, will be drawn inevitably toward the nature-centred beliefs found in Celtic-rooted taboos. Indeed, it can be argued that Paganism and Fatalism meet at a cross-road called Superstition.

The gambling deep-sea trawlermen diced with death. One mistake on the deck or in the wheelhouse and they paid with their lives — no stakes can be higher than that. There can be few work-forces who would willingly enter such a high-risk occupation. Yet Hull's fishing community produced a breed of seafarers able to undertake this perilous Arctic work. Generation after generation, a new wave of trawlerlads flocked to the fish dock. As young boys growing up on Hessle Road they had been saturated in a sea of superstition which made them absorb a fatalistic outlook on life. Another reason for this taboo-bound outlook is that it produced a quick and simple answer to complex and varied questions. Regardless of what we do, we desire to know "Why?". "What caused that effect?" But the cause-and-effect chain in deep-sea trawling is often unknown. Like an iceberg, the menacing part is submerged. A skipper's unanswered questions are endless: Why this violent storm? Why no fish? Why am I fog-bound? Why did I lose my son? Why do other skippers have more luck? Why is the trawler sinking?

Skippers worked their way up from the deck to the wheelhouse. They attended Nautical School (Boulevard) or Trinity House; but generally they were more men of instinct than intellect. Given such a complexity of questions and limited information upon which to find an answer, it was simpler to invoke good or bad luck to explain why something did or did not happen. It is, if you like, a logical use of irrational magic. Nature acts in mysterious ways, so does luck. Therefore, it is relatively easy to account for what is seen to happen in terms of good or bad fortune. If an ominous event (simply overhearing the sacred word 'pig') is seen as the underlying cause of a complex disaster, then the mind can be put at rest and the search for a deeper solution can cease. But in this life-long process it also made that person more open to a fatalistic philosophy. Associated with this went a deep respect for the forces of Nature. So much so that the sea itself becomes personified as a sea god/goddess. A deity whose moods change rapidly from kind to cruel without reason. The sea is vengeful and has to be appeased by rituals, gifts and human sacrifice — thus the *'fear of the gods'* definition of superstition.

On the rational surface, superstitions are silly and nonsensical. But beneath the turbulent waves, savage undercurrents stir. Deep in our irrational emotions, intuitive taboos are essential for our survival as a species. Superstitious beliefs equip us with a daring philosophy to trust in the gods and brave the odds.

**Chapter 35**

## *CONCLUSION*

### FORWARD IN HOPE

POEM: *Hope is a rope to pull us toward tomorrow.* (Alec Gill)

Life on Hessle Road was swept along on a wave of emotion. And the superstitions provided a strong under-current which kept hopes afloat. Nothing comes from nothing (or nonsense, as some would label folk wisdom). Superstitions are saying something. We must learn to listen. In these subconscious signals is a vital message of survival. It is a universal chorus, and relates to the state of being in *'awe of the gods'*. Yet for thousands of years, the folklore has been suppressed by religion and science alike. The powers-that-be have done everything they can to stamp out simple folk belief.

The ordinary people, however, have always been in tune with this ancient rhythm and the inner feelings it reflects. Folk magic continues because it beats in harmony with the suffering soul. Within the hearts of Hull's fishing families flowed the spirit of the sea. The Hessle Roaders floated and foundered on a tide of passion. Their fears flooded and fell as often as the changing tides of the Humber Estuary. The cycles of the sea are seductive, and a ship upon it is vulnerable, especially a side-winder in the Arctic Ocean. Each trawling trip was fraught with uncertainty. An unspoken anxiety ran through the women ashore and the men afloat. It was their closeness to death which gave them such a zest for life. They took each day as it came, helped one another in times of trouble, crammed in lots of fun and joy because they never knew when it would end. They lived for the moment because death could strike in an instant.

The flame of superstition was fanned by the hand of death — it might knock on any door. Not knowing when the call would come caused some to search for the warning signs. This was why the random actions of animals were seen as crucial. Creatures outside mortal control gave clues about future events. The ways of women were particularly attuned to ominous premonitions. Wise women were the guardians of ancient wisdom and perpetuated the superstitions via the oral tradition. They had forebodings of future fatalities. It was the women who took articles of clothing to Spiritualists gatherings. They spread the word of pending disaster. Heightened anxiety was not fuelled by evil, witch-like motives. It was, indirectly, an act of kindness — done in awe of the gods — intended to prepare the community for the worst. It was the way the community coped with the sudden shock of a trawling tragedy. The climate of anxiety was caring and kind in three major ways.

Fatalism is a by-product of superstitious belief. This simple folk philosophy provided 'benefits' for the families in the community and the crews aboard ship. Psychologically, it prepared the trawlermen to face any perilous situation. On one hand, they took dangerous risks confident that their luck would hold.

161

Some put their faith in a lucky talisman or believed that the ship would protect them from a raging sea. On the other hand, when their luck ran out, fatalism created a context of calm acceptance for a noble death at sea — like a Viking warrior. We saw the attitude of brave self-sacrifice in the final words of the skippers of the *Lord Deramore* (H.461), *Lorella* (H.455), *Roderigo* (H.135), and *Ross Cleveland* (H.61). And also in the attitudes of other crew members who read the signs and foresaw their destiny, yet still set sail to accept their lot. Bosun Victor Harbord and second engineer Edward Holmes both had a premonition that the *Endon* (H.161) would be an 'iron coffin'; similar forebodings were felt about the *Girdleness* (H.782), *Kingston Amber* (H.471), and *St. Finbarr* (H.308); and Brian Williams, after the loss of his two brothers Terry and Harry predicted, 'It'll happen to me yu'know". And it did.

By contrast, when the anticipated death at sea did not happen, there could sometimes be a feeling of disappointment. Cat-loving chief engineer Frank Green, who luckily avoided the fatal trip aboard the *Lady Jeanette* (H.466) and other lost trawlers, long held a "gut feeling that he would die at sea". His wife Nancy commented upon his emotional regret at living into old age (75) and knowing that he would die at home in bed (Ch. 17). It could be that mariners have a martyr-like feeling about their mistress the sea. To be claimed by her is, subconsciously, a death of dignity of the highest calling.

Secondly, the climate of anxiety continually prepared families for death within the close-knit fishing community. It does not necessarily make the widow's body-less bereavement easy, painless, tear-less or guilt-less; but the high level of anxiety means that the mechanism of acceptance is already in motion before disaster strikes. Equally, the women around her are better able to understand the distressed widow's plight and provide comfort. A view expressed by one widow of the sea was that, "If you marry a fisherman, at the back of your mind, you half expect that he might not come back". This realistic attitude highlighted how superstitions are an interaction with death.

Living with such uncertainty caused some to search for stability in their daily lives. Again, folk beliefs aided this quest. If things were going well, the feeling arose that nothing must be done to disturb the run of good luck. From this state evolved a 'fear of change'. If an item of clothing was put on the wrong way round, for example, "it must not be *changed* in case you *changed* your luck" (mimic magic again). Neither must the regular taxi driver be changed, nor removing something once placed inside the sea bag. Not emptying a tea-pot once the fishing had started also fell into this category, so does not clearing out the ash-pan at home and, most serious of all, not turning or looking back.

Insight into the third positive effect of living in a community of heightened emotionality is provided by turning the universal 'don't look back' taboo on its head. The indirect message here is to 'only look forward' — it is unlucky to do otherwise. The implication of this is that it is not wise to dwell upon a tragic loss: simply put it down to Fate or bad luck, and then go forward in hope. Acceptance occurs both before and after the loss. Destiny cannot be challenged for that is to defy the gods. The gods are not to be angered, otherwise more punishment will follow. No matter what series of tragedy set a fishing family back, they found an inner strength to keep going forward.

Superstition and survival go hand in hand. The Hessle Roaders are born survivors. They were helped in this by the vitality generated by their folk beliefs. It was their affinity with the Sea and Nature that allowed parallels to be drawn between the ancient Pagan practices and the Hull fishing taboos (Ch. 32). This timeless bond is forged when people, ancient or modern, brave the elements.

The Hessle Roaders are a 'brave' people; yet they themselves are the last to claim this. They cannot. They are prevented from doing so by their superstitious upbringing. They dare not brag or become full of themselves. That 'Tempts Fate', and bad luck will strike them down if they 'get above themselves'. The Celtic blood in them prefers the hint, the allusion, the indirect approach, the subtle suggestion — not the bold, direct statement. The tendency 'not to divulge' is a safeguard against being seen as boastful. It is an intimate part of their *'fear of the gods'* attitude — another subconscious message they have picked up from their taboo-centred culture. Strength in silence.

The folk magic of the Hessle Roaders satisfied a wide range of needs — but the main purpose for each person was day-to-day 'survival'. For the trawlermen at sea, the superstitions bred in them a strong fatalism. They succumbed to death and went down with their ships when all hope was gone. The understanding was, "There's no back door aboard a trawler" — no escape. Theirs was a silent sacrifice of the self to the spirits of the sea.

For a widow, it was the beginning of her hardship. Yet her life-time of folklore knowledge created a subconscious preparation for loss at sea. This high expectation partly softened the blow and partly accelerated the acceptance of her fate. Her father-less children, brought up in these beliefs, were encouraged to go forward in confidence. The hidden message is one of 'letting go' of the past. The dead must be released in order that the living can live life to the full. For everyone in Hull's fishing community, the superstitions and folk magic provided a glimmer of optimism at a time of gloom. After a trawling tragedy, there was always the hope that, with a bit of luck, life would be better and brighter in the future.

*This is a Rainbow Wedding with the bride's maids wearing different coloured dresses – including the superstitious green. Ted Rilatt married Laura McDougall on the 1 October 1934. She was not from a fishing family and so her sister Emily wore green. The wedding had been cancelled four times because Ted was aboard the* **Cape Trafalgar** *(H.918) herring fishing with his skipper dad 'Mad' Rilatt (on left). Around 200 guests were formally invited. But 'Mad' gave an open invitation to all his trawling friends – over 400 people turned up! Green, however, was not unlucky for the Rilatt's who are looking forward to celebrating their 60th anniversary.*
Courtesy Ted & Laura Rilatt.

# REFERENCES

ABRAHAMS, W. H. (1894) *In Flamborough Village and Headland,* (Edited by Rev. Robert Fisher) Hull: William Andrews & Company.

ANSON, Peter (1932) *Fishermen and Fishing Ways*, London: George Harrap & Company.

ANSON, Peter (1965) *Fisher Folk-Lore*, London: Faith Press.

BETZ, Hans (1987) '*Magic in Greco-Roman Antiquity*', — see Eliade, M. —Vol. 9, pp. 93-97.

BIRLEA, Ovidiu (1987) '*Folklore*', — see Eliade, M. — Vol. 5, pp. 363-70.

BLACKCAT (1988) *Encyclopedia of Magic and Superstition*, London: MacDonald & Company.

BREWER, Ebenezer (1990) *Brewer's Dictionary of Phrase and Fable*, (First published 1870 — 14th Edition by Ivor Evans) London: Cassell.

CAVENDISH, Richard (1980) *Man, Myth and Magic: Encyclopedia of the Supernatural*, London: Purnell (monthly magazines built into volumes — lent by Robert Ramsbottom).

COLLINS (1990) *Concise Dictionary Plus*, London: William Collins & Sons.

CONSIDINE (1989) *Van Nostrand's Scientific Encyclopedia*, (7th Edition) New York: Van Nostrand Reinhold.

CROWTHER, Ernest (1987) *Worse Things Happen at Sea: An Autobiography of Early Life in Hull*, Hull: Malet Lambert Local History Original — Volume 36.

DUNNIGAN, Ann (1987) '*Fish*', — see Eliade, M. — Vol. 5, pp. 346-47.

EDWARDS, Gillian (1974) *Hobgoblin and Sweet Puck: Fairy Names and Nature*, London: Geoffrey Bles.

ELIADE, Mircea (1987, Editor) *The Encyclopedia of Religion,* Vols. 1-16, New York: Macmillan/Collier (around one dozen articles are cited from this reference under each author's name. An excellent source for anyone studying beliefs).

ELLIS, Peter (1987) *A Dictionary of Irish Mythology*, London: Constable.

ENCYCLOPÆDIA JUDAICA (1971) '*Pig*', pp. 506-507, Jerusalem: Keter Publishing House Limited.

FARRAR, Janet & Stewart (1987) *The Witches' Goddess: The Feminine Principle of Divinity*, London: Robert Hale.

FLEMING, Elizabeth (1934) '*Egg-shells*' In *The Golden Wonder Book for Children*, (Edited by John Crossland & J. M. Parrish) London: Odhams Press Limited.

FRAZER, James (1922) *The Golden Bough: A Study in Magic and Religion*, (Abridged Edition) London: Macmillan/Papermac.

FREUD, Sigmund (1913) *Totem and Taboo*, (Translated by James Strachey, 1950) London: Routledge & Kegan Paul.

GILL, Alec (1987) *Hessle Road: A Photographer's View of Hull's Trawling Days,* Beverley: Hutton Press.

GILL, Alec (1989) *Lost Trawlers of Hull: Nine Hundred Losses 1835-1987*, Beverley: Hutton Press.

GILL, Alec (1991) *Good Old Hessle Road: Stories of Hull's Trawling and Community Life*, Beverley: Hutton Press.

GILL, Alec & SARGEANT, Gary (1985) *Village Within A City: The Hessle Road Fishing Community of Hull*, Hull: Hull University Press.

GIMBUTAS, Marija (1987) '*Prehistoric Religions*', — see Eliade, M. — Vol. 11, pp. 505-15.

GUERBER, H. A. (1908) *Myths of the Norsemen*, London: George Harrap & Company.

HAINING, Peter (1979) *Superstitions*, London: Sidgwick & Jackson.

HOLE, Christina (1979) *A Dictionary of British Folk Customs*, London: Paladin/Granada Publishing.

HOLLAND-MARTIN, Deric (1969) *Trawler Safety: Final Report of the Committee of Inquiry into Trawler Safety*, London: HMSO.

HOUGHTON, Patricia (1981) *As Mad as a March Hare: The World of Proverbs*, Poole, Dorset: Javelin Books.

HUTCHINSON, Albert (1938) *Thrills of the Northern Trawl*, London: Hutchinson & Company.

JAHODA, Gustav (1969) *The Psychology of Superstition*, London: Allen Lane/Penguin.

LEHANE, Brendan (1984) *Wizards and Witches*, Amsterdam: Time-Life Books — The Enchanted World Series.

MacCANA, Proinsias (1987) '*Celtic Religion*', — see Eliade, M. — Vol. 3, pp. 148-66.

MAPLE, Eric (1980) '*Cat*', — see Cavendish, R. — pp. 417-21.

MATTHEWS, John & Caitlin (1988) *The Aquarian Guide to British and Irish Mythology*, Wellingborough: The Aquarian Press.

METZGER, Bruno & Isobel (1962) *The Oxford Concise Concordance: To The Revised Standard Version of the Holy Bible*, London: Oxford University Press.

MIDDLETON, John (1987) '*MAGIC: Theories of Magic*' — see Eliade, M. —Vol. 9, pp. 81-115.

NEW ENCYCLOPÆDIA BRITANNICA (1979) Micropædia, (30 Volumes), 15th Edition, Chicago: Encyclopædia Britannica.

NICHOLSON, John (1890) *Folk Lore of East Yorkshire*, Hull: A. Brown & Sons (Re-printed 1973 by E. P. Pub).

O'NEIL, Mary (1987) '*Superstition*', — see Eliade, M. — Vol. 14, pp. 163-66.

OPIE, Iona & TATEM, Moira (1989) *A Dictionary of Superstitions*, Oxford: Oxford University Press.

POPHAM, Hugh (1957) *Cape of Storms: Trawling off the Coast of North Russia*, London: Rupert Hart-Davis.

PRESTON, James (1987) '*Goddess Worship: An Overview*', — see Eliade, M. —Vol. 6, pp. 35-59.

RADFORD, E. & M. A., (1974) *Encyclopædia of Superstitions*, (Revised by Christina Hole) London: Book Club Association.

RAINE, Kathleen (1985) *Defending Ancient Springs*, Ipswich: Golgonooza Press.

RAPPOPORT, Angelo (1930) *Superstitions of Sailors*, London: Stanley Paul.

READER'S DIGEST (1977) *Folklore, Myths and Legends of Britain*, London: Reader's Digest Association.

RHEA, Nicholas (1985) *Constable by the Sea*, London: Robert Hale.

ROBERTS, David (1993) 'The Iceman: Lone Voyager from the Copper Age', *National Geographical Magazine*, Vol. 183 (No. 6), June, pp. 36-67.

ROSS, Anne (1974) *Pagan Celtic Britain: Studies in Iconography and Tradition*, London: Cardinal/Sphere Books.

ROSS, Anne (1980) *'Celts'*, — see Cavendish, R. — pp. 438-44.

SIMONS, G. L. (1973) *Sex and Superstition*, London: Abelard-Schuman.

SPAVEN, Mary (1984) *Superstitions Among the Fishing Community of Hull*, An unpublished 32-item list displayed at the Hull Heritage Centre.

STEAD, I. M. (1979) *The Arras Culture*, York: The Yorkshire Philosophical Society.

STONE, Merlin (1987) *'Goddess Worship in the Ancient Near East'*, — see Eliade, M. — Vol. 6, pp. 45-49.

THURSTON, Herbert (1933) *Superstition: A Backward Glance over Nineteen Centuries*, London: Centurary Press.

TOLKIEN, J. R. R. (1975) *Sir Gawain and the Green Knight*, London: Unwin Paperbacks.

VALIENTE, Doreen (1975) *Natural Magic*, London: Guild Publishing.

VILLIERS, Alan (1956) *Posted Missing: The Story of Ships Lost Without Trace in Recent Years*, London: Hodder & Stoughton.

WAGNER, Roy (1987) *'Taboo'*, — see Eliade, M. — Vol. 14, pp. 233-36.

WALKER, Benjamin (1977) *Encyclopaedia of Esoteric Man*, London: Routledge & Kegan Paul.

WARING, Philippa (1978) *A Dictionary of Omens and Superstitions*, London: Souvenir Press.

WILLIS, Jerome (1937) *The Last Adventurers*, London: Hurst & Blackett Limited.

WUNDT, Wilhelm (1921) *Elements of Folk Psychology*, London: George Allen & Unwin.

YUSA, Mickiko (1987) *'Chance'*, — see Eliade, M. — Vol. 3, pp. 192-96.

ZUESSE, Evan (1987) *'Divination'*, — see Eliade, M. — Vol. 4, pp. 375-82.

# INDEX

Superstitions are performed by people in different places aboard specific trawlers. This index reflects that process. The index is set out in six main sections:

* SUPERSTITIONS
* FAMILY NAMES
*PLACES
* SHIPS plus TRAWLER OWNERS
* AUTHORS plus NEWSPAPERS
* CONCEPTS

## SUPERSTITIONS

## FAMILY NAMES

## PLACES

## SHIPS
### (plus Trawler Owners)

171

## Trawler Owners

## AUTHORS
### (plus Newspapers)

## Newspapers

## CONCEPTS